THE MEANING OF
TRANSCENDENCE

American Academy of Religion
Dissertation Series

edited by
Wendell Dietrich

Number 35

THE MEANING OF
TRANSCENDENCE
A Heideggerian Reflection
by
Robert P. Orr

Robert P. Orr
The Meaning of Transcendence: A Heideggerian Reflection

Scholars Press

Distributed by
Scholars Press
101 Salem Street
PO Box 2268
Chico, California 95927

The Meaning of Transcendence
A Heideggerian Reflection

Robert P. Orr

Library of Congress Cataloging in Publication Data

Orr, Robert P
    The meaning of transcendence.

    (Dissertation series–American Academy of Religion ; no.
35 ISSN 0145-272X)
    Originally presented as the author's thesis, Vanderbilt
University, 1979.
    Bibliography: p.
    1. Heidegger, Martin, 1889-1976. 2.   Transcendence
(Philosophy) 3.   Meaning (Philosophy) I.Title. II. Series:
American Academy of Religion. Dissertation series–American
Academy of Religion ; no. 35.
B3279.H49077   1980   193   80-12872
ISBN 0-89130-407-X
ISBN 0-89130-408 (pbk.)

Printed in the United States of America
1   2   3   4   5   6
Edwards Brothers, Inc.
Ann Arbor, MI 48106

CONTENTS

64874

PREFACE

The following dissertation represents a culmination, of
sorts, of six years of intermittent meandering within the
Heideggerian provenance. That meandering, however, has not
been completely random and directionless inasmuch as it has
been loosely guided by the following question: How can one
understand the foundations of religious experience and the
affirmations that result therefrom within the purview of
Heideggerian thought? My own answer to this question, insofar
as I can formulate such an answer at this time, is contained in
the following pages. Whatever worth such an answer may have,
let alone the question that underlies it, is an issue for others
to resolve as they see fit.

I wish to acknowledge the aid and support of several persons
to whom I owe much in connection with the writing of this work.
To begin with, I must acknowledge a debt of gratitude to my
adviser, Dr. Peter C. Hodgson, whose advice and friendly criti-
cism have undoubtedly improved whatever value these pages may
exhibit. In addition, I owe much to Dr. Charles E. Scott who
inspired my interest in Heidegger in the first place, and provided for me an initial entree into this difficult realm of
thought. In this same connection I must also mention my debt to
Dr. Edward Farley, who stimulated interest in the more general
field of phenomenology and its relation to theology. In addition to these three, I wish to make mention of the very important
support and encouragement that I received while writing this work
from several friends, Dr. Carl Walters and Robin Walters, as well
as Dr. Michael McLain, Barry Goldberg, my brother Philip and
sister-in-law Carolyn, and my parents, Dr. William Orr and
Mildred Orr. Finally, but certainly not least in order of importance, I wish to thank my typist Terri Tesar, who typed these
pages diligently, enabling me to meet some pressing deadlines.

One final note. Throughout the ensuing pages, I introduce
the English translation of German texts with the abbreviation
E.T.

vii

CHAPTER I

INTRODUCTION: THE QUESTION OF TRANSCENDENCE

*The Meaning of Transcendence as such Versus
the Concept of the Transcendence of God*

The aim of this work as a whole is to inquire into the
meaning of transcendence as such. Ordinarily, the term "transcendence" is taken to name the state of being attributable to
God relative to the state of being of the world. But the aim
of this work is not framed in terms of the question of the
transcendence of God. The aim is not to advance still one more
interpretation of the concept of God's transcendence, nor to
attempt one more clarification of the interrelation of the two
contrasting concepts: transcendence/immanence. Instead, we
have formulated our aim as follows: to attempt in thought to
encounter the meaning of transcendence *as such*.

By speaking in this way of transcendence, we intend to
introduce at the outset a distinction between the *meaning* of
transcendence as such and the *concept* of the transcendence of
God. Although the justification for drawing this distinction
can become fully apparent only in the course of the total work,
some initial indication of the need for it should be stated
here. And in order to do this, we must first attempt to clarify
the distinction itself.

One side of this distinction, namely the concept of the
transcendence of God, is clear enough that little needs to be
said in order to identify it initially. This concept can be
adequately characterized as the concept of the *irreducible otherness* of the divine being relative to the total world available
for direct human experience.[1] In other words, the concept of
the transcendence of God is the concept of the *relation* between
one distinguishable being (God) and the totality of all other
beings which together constitute the world of human experience.

In contrast to this *concept* of the transcendence of God,
we propose to speak of the *meaning* of transcendence as such.
The distinction that we are drawing thus involves the distinction

1

between concept and meaning. In the sense that we are using
the term here, "concept" means a structure or form of thought
through which a number of particular things or instances can be
grasped in their commonality. By speaking of the meaning of
transcendence as such, we wish to avoid any impression that we
are inquiring into the concept of transcendence. To be sure,
one can speak of the concept of transcendence in the general
and abstract sense of "standing outside or beyond." And of
course, one can apply this indifferent form of difference to
the specific instance of God's purported otherness with respect
to the world of human experience taken as a whole. But this
empty concept of transcendence, as well as its application to
the particular relation of God and the world, is *not* our subject
of attention here.

In what way, then, is the phrase "the meaning of transcendence as such" to be taken? In order to answer this question,
we need to attend to what the phrase itself says. In this
phrase, three components may be found: "meaning," "transcendence," and "as such." The second of these components, the word
"transcendence" itself, is the center of the phrase and as such
is what conveys the intended subject matter. Accordingly, we
will soon turn our attention directly to this word and to its
meaning. But in addition to this second and central component,
there are also the other two components which tell *how* this
subject-matter is to be received. In the first place, the term
"meaning" tells how the subject-matter makes itself a matter of
human concern. By speaking of the *meaning* of transcendence as
such, we indicate that transcendence is a matter of concern not
in the manner of a concept (a formal generality applicable to
several particulars), but as a singularity that has the concrete-
ness appropriate to a meaning as such. In addition, the term
"meaning" also serves to indicate that transcendence is not a
particular something after the fashion of things which appear in
their own mode of self-identical presence. To say that we seek
the meaning of transcendence is to say that we do not predelin-
eate transcendence as either particular thing or conceptual
universal. Yet this is not to say that transcendence is here
taken as "mere meaning" and thus as somehow less "real" and
hence less important than are tangible, particular things.

Indeed, one of the burdens of this work is to maintain that
meaning is more "real" in the twofold sense of more fundamental
and more intrinsically compelling than discrete, particular
things can in principle be.

Because transcendence is to be investigated here under the
rubric of "meaning," an interpretation of meaning is called for.
Accordingly, in Chapter II of this work an extended interpretation of meaning will be given. For the present, it must suffice
merely to state that meaning will be characterized as "claim,"
as "allowance," as "grant," and in addition as an essential
"withholding" *of itself* from all coming into appearance *as something*. To foreshadow what will be developed later, we now
offer the following: Meaning is *claim* in that it is the fundamental transpiring of that which "lays claim" to human awareness,
and in so doing actually institutes such awareness. Meaning is
allowance in that it is the transpiring and prevailing of the
essential "place" within which anything is first allowed to show
itself in its particularity. Meaning is *grant* in that it
emerges as gift to be received rather than as human creation or
as a mere instrument employed in the service of some human
function (i.e., signification). And finally, meaning is a *self-
withholding* in that meaning itself is not such as to make an
appearance or to come forth *as* something in particular. To
speak of the *meaning* of transcendence as such is thus to suggest
that transcendence concerns man not in the manner of something
which stands forth in its appearance as something, but is rather
a claim which grants itself to human being in such a way as to
make allowance in a strictly fundamental sense for the coming-
to-appearance of something as something.

The third component of our phrase, the "as such," tells how
the subject-matter of transcendence is to be entertained as a
matter for thought. To speak of the meaning of transcendence
as such means that we must attempt to permit this subject-matter
to enter thought strictly on its own terms as it gives itself
for thought. In order to do this, one must remove oneself from
the hegemony of inherited structures and forms of thought, and
become fully *receptive* in an attending which does not prescribe
its own direction but rather allows itself to be directed by the
self-giving of the subject-matter itself. The manner in which

we are to entertain the subject-matter of transcendence is thus
phenomenological and hermeneutical. Phenomenological in the
sense of a strict attending to the subject-matter itself without
prior delimitation of the subject matter, and hermeneutical in
the sense of the reception of a "message" which claims us for
itself.

As we stated earlier, the second component of our phrase,
namely the term "transcendence" itself, is the center of the
phrase and is thus what conveys the subject-matter. What, then,
does this word say? The English word "transcendence" is a
nominative derived from the Latin verb $transcend\bar{o}$.[2] This verb,
in turn, is based on the root $scand\bar{o}$, an old Latin root which
is derived from the Indo-European root $skand$. This root, as
well as the Latin $scand\bar{o}$, means "to climb, to ascend by march-
ing." In addition to the meaning of "to climb," $scand\bar{o}$ also
means "to measure by its feet," "to set a measure," as in the
English verb "to scan." In the Latin root $scand\bar{o}$, this latter
meaning occurs solely in reference to grammar, as in "to scan
the feet of a poem." However, one can understand the relation
of these two meanings by considering the footprints that are
left behind during a climb. These footprints are measures,
instituted in the act of climbing, which are deposited in the
imprint as fixed delineations of the effort of climbing as well
as of the nature and distance of the terrain traversed. Out of
the fluidity and dynamism of the climb there is left behind the
fixity of a measure which, nevertheless, is but a frozen afterimage of the actual occurrence of the march. Thus, "to climb"
and "to scan, to measure by its feet," can be seen to have a
common source of meaning.

The verb $transcend\bar{o}$ prefixes to the verb $scand\bar{o}$ the preposi-
tion "$trans$," which means simply "across." Thus, $transcend\bar{o}$
means "to climb across, to climb over." Recalling the derivative
meaning of $scand\bar{o}$ in the grammatical sense of "to scan," one may
also hear in $transcend\bar{o}$ a hint of the meaning of "to climb over
fixed measure," "to pass beyond that which is measured out."
In any event, the Latin $transcendo$ also means "to surmount."

From this we may say that the English verb "to transcend"
has the primary meaning of "to pass over," "to go beyond or
above," either with respect to a physical obstacle or with

respect to some non-physical limit. Thus the primary meaning
of the English verb is to pass beyond a fixed boundary or
measure of some sort or other. The noun "transcendence" would
thus also have the primary sense of such passing-beyond.

This primary, verbal meaning is then extended to include
a secondary meaning, namely any "passing-beyond" or increase
with respect to some quality or descriptive property. In this
sense, "to transcend" means "to surpass, to excel, to exceed."
And from this extension, the verb comes to mean "to be transcendent" in the sense of *achieved* excellence.

From this dictionary account, two rather different tenden-
cies of meaning may be detected. On the one hand, the term
signifies a kind of movement or dynamism in which some fixed
boundary, limit or measure is traversed, left behind. In this
sense, "transcendence" is primarily verbal, entailing a movement
beyond whatever lies as a fixed limit in the path of the movement.

On the other hand, the second tendency of meaning extends
the basic sense of "movement beyond" to include the surpassing
that is characteristic of qualitative increase or increase in
value. Such an extension now involves not "movement beyond" as
such, but rather the relative comparison of stable positions and
values. Thus in this extension, the exertion, the dynamism
inherent in the verbal sense of "movement beyond" recedes and is
supplanted by relatively static relations of superiority with
respect to some quality.

A further extension of meaning builds upon this second
tendency. Relative superiority can be replaced by absolute
superiority. When this is done, the term then comes to designate a static and perfected condition of excellence. Here there
is no longer any dynamism, exertion or occurrent movement, but
rather the fully achieved state of completed perfection. This,
of course, is the state purportedly fulfilled by the God of
traditional Western theism.

Our study of the meaning of the term "transcendence" reveals
that the primary meaning conveyed is "passage beyond fixed
boundary, measure, limit." Only later does the term come to
bear the sense of "achieved excellence or perfection." Based
partly on the assumption that the initial emergence of a word-
meaning is likely to be more pregnant or more thought-worthy

than later, more refined and functionally specific senses that
a word conveys, we will take as our clue the earlier, dynamic
meaning of "transcendence." Accordingly, we will be guided in
our inquiry by this initial bearing: "transcendence" names
passing-beyond with respect to what is fixed, determinate, delimited. Our task is to try to discover how best to give
thought to transcendence, understood preliminarily in this way.

The Need for an Inquiry into the Meaning
of Transcendence as Such

Hopefully enough has been said to introduce the distinction
we wish to suggest between the meaning of transcendence as such,
on the one hand, and conceptualizations of the transcendence of
God, on the other. But we have not yet addressed the question
of the need for such a distinction. Of what importance is it?
In what way is it required, and for what?

In our recent cultural past, it had become something of a
dogma to claim that the notion of transcendence is meaningless.
According to this dogma, man no longer needs the illusion of a
more abundant reality lying beyond the horizon of this reality
which we know immediately as our world. Human beings have on
the whole come to rest their concerns, hopes and fears squarely
within this present world. And of what sort is this present
world? Again, to follow the orthodoxy of our recent cultural
past, this world is taken to be thoroughly secular, exhibiting
no transparent openings to a realm of sacred otherness, nor even
any signposts which can be accredited as legitimately pointing
forward to such a realm. Thus the conclusion followed that the
term "transcendence" can no longer bear meaning that is in any
way relevant to the thoroughgoing secularity of contemporary
life and its self-understanding.

To be sure, there is now in evidence a weakening of this
recent cultural orthodoxy. The widespread interest in the
occult, in astrology, in purportedly inexplicable phenomena of
various sorts, etc., indicates that there is a growing dissatis-
faction with the prevalent picture of reality as wholly immanent
in everyday human experience. People seem to have a sense or
feeling that there is more in being, and more that may concern

man, than what is to be encountered in everyday experience. But
be this as it may, there does not yet seem to be any fully acceptable ways of interpreting this sense of "something more." Hence,
there are still no culturally approved ways of including "transcendence" within the common discourse of life. The prevalent
understanding of human life and of that which truly concerns
human life would still seem to be one that excludes transcendence
as a real and important element.

In theological circles, this recent cultural rejection of
transcendence has been reflected in discussions of the loss of
transcendence in our Western self-understanding. In some
instances, as, for example, the radical theologians of the "death
of God" movement, this supposed loss was accepted as fact and
theologians were urged to pick up the pieces of their heritage
by translating all traditional language of transcendence into
language which would illuminate man's new self-understanding and
the "higher" secular possibilities now found to await him. In
other instances, attempts were made to discover genuinely within
secular culture itself some hidden presence of transcendence.[3]
But whatever the merit of these various theological responses
to the increasing secularism of modern culture, there has not yet
been provided a way of thinking which would really allow for a
genuine acknowledgment of transcendence as something that inescap-
ably concerns man. Consequently, the issue of the importance of
transcendence as a matter for inquiry remains at the very least
unresolved, and in the opinion of many positively eradicated as
a genuine subject for human questioning.

One of the burdens of this work is to show that recent cultural orthodoxy notwithstanding, the essential meaning of transcendence has not simply disappeared altogether as an element
having importance for contemporary life. We will maintain that
Western culture has in fact not lived thorugh a loss of transcendence per se, but rather has experienced merely the demise of a
certain way of thinking about transcendence, a mode of thinking
which could entertain the meaning of transcendence only in terms
of that which comes forth in self-identity and hence as able to
stand forth into an available appearance. It is our contention
that although most if not all of traditional Western thought has
been bound to an ontology which understands being in terms of

that which might possibly come into appearance as what it itself
is, i.e., an ontology of self-identical presence, we now have in
the writings of Martin Heidegger and others some hints of a way
of thinking which does not understand everything ahead of time
in terms of such self-identical presence. And it is by means of
this new way of thinking that we wish to raise anew the question
of the meaning of transcendence.

Thus far we have merely suggested that we wish to separate
the traditional manner of thinking with respect to transcendence
from the question of the meaning of transcendence as such. But
this in itself does not establish any need for raising this
latter question anew. In order to address squarely the issue
of such need, we will now attempt to outline the way in which
the traditional ontology of self-identical presence gives rise
to a corresponding way of thinking with respect to transcendence.
And then we will attempt to show that the modern thought-orienta-
tion of man requires *both* the rejection of the traditional way
of thinking with respect to transcendence, *and* a new questioning
into the meaning of transcendence as such.

As we have said above, the prevalent manner of thinking
found in the Western tradition understands "to be" as *attained
presence*, which in turn means self-showing in appearance, coming
forth as self-identical in the availability of an appearance.
But in order for the *being* of anything to be understood as self-
identical presence, this being must already be understood as the
ability to attain to self-coincidence, the ability to attain to
a self-containment which in turns sustains the *possibility* of
self-showing in the availability of an appearance. In the traditional ontology of presence, then, being must itself mean self-
coincidence, the "power" of self-coincidence, the pervasive
thrust into self-coincidence.

This traditional understanding of "to be" can now be applied
to transcendence. As we have seen, the basic meaning of the
term is "surpassing" in the sense of "passing beyond boundary,
measure, fixed limit." How can this meaning be understood within
the scope of being, understood as self-coincidence, the power of
self-identical presence? The only way that surpassing can itself
be thought within this scope is in terms of the absolute *self-
sufficiency* of a self-coincident self-showing in appearance. Let

us now attempt to elaborate this claim. If "to be" means to
attain a self-coincidence which in turns sustains the possibility
of a standing-forth, in self-identity, into the availability of
an appearance, then limit, boundary, the finite measurableness
of the definite all emerge in the *non-self-sufficiency* of self-
showing fully and completely to sustain the *availability* of its
own appearance. The very definiteness or determinateness of
particular self-showing is precisely a *need* for the external,
for that which lies beyond its own self-contained identity. To
be determinate in self-showing, or to be particular, is thus to
be unable from within internal self-coincidence to found the
possibility of self-appearance. Self-appearance is a need for
the external, for the delimitedness which emerges with the
division into internal and external, and for the *perspective*
which first accrues in otherness and which grounds the possibility of perception, of seeing something *as something*, i.e., as a
particular sort of thing. But to the extent that self-appearance
is *need for the external*, the internal identity (self-coincidence)
of something is insufficient to account for the availability of
its own appearance. Such availability arises only in the differentiation of otherness from self-identity, in the emergence of
perspective in such otherness, and in the correlative emergence
of "seeing as" which attends perspective.

    We can now see that transcendence, if it is thought in terms
of the traditional ontology of presence, can mean *surpassing
fixed limit* only if it also means overcoming the need, the in-
sufficiency, of particular self-showing in appearance. Transcendence must accordingly mean the absolute self-sufficiency of its
own presence, the absolute self-sufficiency of its self-coincident self-showing in appearance. But how is this a possibility
for thought? One can think such self-sufficiency only in terms
of the absolute *self-completion* of self-showing in appearance.
This means that the being (power of self-coincidence) of transcendence is the absolute appearance *to itself* of that which is
utterly in appearance without need of the differentiation into
internal and external, and hence without the delimitation entailed by otherness and externality. Transcendence is thus
traditionally understood as perfect self-completion, the
perfection of presence in the sense of the elimination of all

need for the external, utterly self-sustained and self-contained
appearance to itself.[4] On the basis of this thinking rests our
traditional notions of infinity, final fulfillment, the majesty
of God, the *lack* in which the available world of finite determination is deemed to suffer, etc. In short, the traditional
understanding of transcendence based upon the ontology of self-
identical presence (the thrust into self-coincidence) is *utter
self-consummation*.

It is indeed a short step from the utter self-consummation
of transcendence to the rift between transcendence, on the one
hand, and the world of determination, of need for the external,
on the other. Thus the overwhelming implication of the traditional thinking of transcendence is some form of *separateness*
dividing transcendence from *the human world*. Separateness, otherness, becomes the very hallmark of transcendence as it is traditionally thought.

It is undoubtedly fair to state that this last feature of
the traditional notion of transcendence provides the key to
understanding the modern cultural rejection of transcendence.
Transcendence has failed to find a place within modern culture
precisely because modern self-understanding tends to reject the
meaningfulness (significant impingement upon life) of the separate, the wholly other. And there is good reason for this rejection, although it may yet be true that what is rejected is
separateness and not transcendence as such.

Why has transcendence as separateness from the environing
world been rejected as a member in good standing of the pantheon
of culturally sanctioned meanings? This rejection, it is fair
to say, follows directly upon a development in the understanding
of how human beings are related to their world. How has this
relation been experienced, and in what way has it changed?

At one time it was a widespread experience that although
one lived *in* the world about one, nevertheless one did not
really belong *to* the surrounding world, nor it to oneself. The
relation of human being to the world was experienced as *accidental*. According to this experience it is merely an accident
that I find myself in this world about me--I could be situated
in a radically different context and still remain me--and the
same can be said, *mutatis mutandis*, of the world.

If it can be said that this is how the relation of human
being to the world was once experienced, it can also be said
that the rise of the so-called modern period in the West is marked
by a noticeable transformation of the way that this relation is
experienced. What took place in this transformation was a shift
from the experience of world-relatedness as accidental to the
experience of world-relatedness as *essential* to the very determination of human being. As a result of this shift, moreover, the
groundplan of that which can be found to impact upon human life
is changed in two significant ways. First, the environing world
is now experienced not as an accidental accoutrement of one's
being, but rather as the situation to which one necessarily and
essentially belongs. Thus the world can no longer be experienced
as *essentially* alien to human being but is experienced instead
as belonging to us and we to it (for better or for worse, one
might be tempted to add). Secondly, the experience of human
being as somehow *discrete* in relation to the world and as essentially capable of "holding its own" irrespective of the world
is also no longer possible. Whether it was as soul, as pure
reason, as will or as pure center of appetite and desire that
the supposed discreteness of human being was catalogued and
interpreted, the thrust of modern understanding is away from
discreteness altogether. In its place is the experience of
human beings as directly constituted by one's relations to and
in the world. In this light, human being is now understood as
the product of worldly conditions, worldly experiences, worldly
interrelations. One *is* not, except as one is built up out of a
unique set and pattern of worldly relations whose intersection,
moreover, *defines* one's personal center (a center which thus
cannot stand on its own independently of its world-relatedness).
One can see the prevalence of this understanding of human being
in relation to the world in the convergence of sociological
observation, depth psychological insight and certain schools of
philosophical thinking.

One can perhaps condense this understanding of human being
in relation to the world by saying that human being is experienced
as *owning* the world, and vice versa.[5] On the basis of this
experience, a primary impulse of human being must accordingly be
to come to own the world about one, that is, to consciously

appropriate it as one's own. And to be sure, much that human
beings do can now be interpreted as attempts to accomplish this
appropriation, an appropriation which is already ours by right.

It should be fairly obvious at this point that the overall
human task of coming to own the world stands in stark opposition
to any continued adherence to the notion of a transcendent home
for human being that is separate and apart from the world as a
whole. This notion is simply not a very viable one if in fact
the meaning of human being is to be found in its world-relatedness. Consequently, the more that human beings find themselves
drawn into the task of world-appropriation, the less significant
will they find the notion of a separate, transcendent reality to
be. And in fact, the demise of the experienced meaningfulness
of any transcendent reality is due precisely to the current
cultural sovereignty of the task of world-appropriation. On
this basis, then, the recent cultural rejection of transcendence
can now be readily interpreted.

If we have succeeded in showing how the recent rejection of
transcendence has come about, and if we wish to assent to the
understanding of human being which lies at the heart of this
rejection, why do we persist, nevertheless, in attempting to
raise anew the question of the meaning of transcendence? The
answer is this: According to our interpretation, what has been
rejected in the turn to the task of world-appropriation is
transcendence in the sense of a reality separate from the world
as a whole. We wish to concur in the general cultural estimation
that such a purported reality can no longer be experienced as
having any significant impact upon human being. However, we do
not concur in the assumed identification of transcendence as
such with this notion of a separate reality. Might it not be the
case that the meaning of transcendence as such is other than a
reality separated in principle (i.e., by its own utter self-
consummation) from the world?

In order to show that this is indeed correct, we may appeal
again to the root meaning of the word "transcendence" and in
addition to a certain primal human phenomenon. As we have seen,
the root meaning conveyed by the term "transcendence" is *not*
"separate reality" but "surpassing fixed limit, boundary, determination." On the face of it, therefore, it would seem possible

to inquire into the meaning of such surpassing without presupposing that the goal of such inquiry is somehow *beyond* the
parameters of the world-arena of direct experience and thus
separate from the world *in toto*.

In addition to this hint derived from the word itself,
there is also a primal human phenomenon which perhaps can best
be characterized as the phenomenon of *depth*. To speak of "depth"
is to draw a contrast between depth and surface. The phenomenon
of surface in our sense can be indicated as the totality of all
everyday experiences with things, other persons, projects, ideas,
functions, etc., all of which fit into an overarching pattern of
busyness and industry. This pattern, in turn, provides the
context within which what is ordinarily deemed meaningful may be
determined. The phenomenon of surface is thus the phenomenon
of a seemingly unsurpassable context of purposiveness whose
individual purposes, moreover, are ultimately subordinated to
the aim toward creative activity for its own sake, industry for
the sake of industry.

In contrast to this, the phenomenon of depth is encountered
at first only during momentary lapses in the otherwise continuous droning of the hum of purposive industry. In comparison to
the surface, and beheld from its vantage-point, the phenomenon
of depth at first appears to be merely the lack of purpose, the
lack of any means and ends structure, and hence the lack of the
tangibility which is manifest as cause and effect. Such a lack
must indeed be estimated as illusion if interpreted in terms of
the surface. Only the purposive, that which fits into the
schema of means and ends, cause and effect, can be real, non-
illusory. Viewed from within the rule of the surface, therefore,
depth is *merely* the negative, and thus antipathetic to human
life.

However one can turn toward the phenomenon of depth in such
a way as to suspend the rule of the surface. In this instance
one slips inside the momentary lapse in the drone of purposiveness and attempts to experience how it is within the lapse. This
lapse does indeed occur. However, one cannot jump at once into
a description of this phenomenon in its purity. One must rather
approach the pure phenomenon by describing the journey from the
surface into the depth.

One begins at the surface, where all is connected in a continuous fabric of interwoven purposes. To be caught up in this
fabric is the usual way that human world-relatedness is lived
out. But occasionally this fabric unravels just enough to allow
an elusive experience which is marked by a dearth of the customary purposiveness and hence of the customary significances. In
this first step toward the phenomenon of depth, the everyday
realities are present in disconnection from the usual means/ends
patterns into which they otherwise fit. The experience is thus
one of discontinuity, alienation, strangeness. There is a
distinct loss of significance and meaning--the meaning peculiar
to surface purposiveness which occurs as something points beyond
itself in some schema of means and ends. In this loss, things
are experienced as devoid of the meaning pertaining to the instru-
mentality of means for an end, and thus as nonsignificant.
Things point neither behind them to causes or to prior purposes
which they have fulfilled, nor ahead of them to future goals
which they will be instrumental in securing. They simply stand
in isolation, as themselves, in stark temporal disconnectedness.

The second step in the journey toward depth is the change
in the experience of self. In the first step, one finds oneself
drawn away from the ordinarily ubiquitous fabric of mundane
purpose. One is thus drawn into one's own center, and into an
experience of self which to some extent parallels the shifted
experience of things in that here the self is experienced as
dislodged from its customary involvements. The usual experience
of self is the experience of a relatively stable albeit dynamic
set of specific aims, projects and intentions which are fed by
memories, concrete expectations, and a general subliminal confi-
dence in one's proven capabilities and aptitudes. This self is
very much interwoven with things and other persons which serve
as the instruments of and collaborators in (and/or obstacles to)
the attainment of the self's defining aims. However, when the
purposive fabric unravels, this experience of the self begins to
dissipate as well. There is here an experience of self-dissolu-
tion, which is announced and borne by the anxiety of self-loss.
And this anxiety reveals that in the moment of purposive lapse,
the self which projects aims into the future and in that projection collects past memories into its tensiveness simply is no

more. The tensiveness which draws the past into future through
present purpose is relaxed. But the surface self is the same as
this tensiveness, and so it evaporates. In this relaxation of
purposive tensility, the self is utterly undefined, and correlatively the defined self expires. Anxiety and loss of situated-
ness prevail in the vacuum of the self's loss of definition.

The final step in this journey toward depth is a movement
which carries beyond the sheer negativity of the anxiety of
self-loss. As mere loss and vacuum this anxiety is dispelled
when one's being is discovered to be located beyond the situated
self, beyond the context of the tensile self of mundane purposiveness. When one begins to discover this nonsituated location of
one's being, one is confronting the phenomenon of depth, and
begins to merge into this phenomenon. For this reason we speak
of depth as a primal human phenomenon.

It is undoubtedly easier to characterize the phenomenon of
depth negatively, that is by saying what it is not, than positively in terms of definite attributes. The phenomenon of depth
eludes, as we have seen, the tensing of time into the vector of
purpose. Because of this it is a non-volitional phenomenon
insofar as volition itself is grounded in this tensing of time,
occurring as purposive vector. One can also say that the
phenomenon of depth is empty of customary significance (although
not, as we maintain, of meaning in any absolute sense). Ordinary
things and customary interactions consequently are found not to
impinge upon the phenomenon of depth.

We could perhaps continue this *via negativa* account of the
phenomenon of depth, but instead we elect to cut off any further
consideration of it. The reason for this is that we have said
enough to be able now to show what we construe to be the need
for raising anew the question of the meaning of transcendence as
such. The term "transcendence" says "surpassing fixed limit,
measure, determination." But we have already indicated that in
the journey toward depth, there is a movement beyond, a surpassing, with respect to the self that is measured by particular
aims and purposes, and also with respect to the ordinary context
of things which are instrumental to those purposes. The surpassing here indicated is thus a surpassing of the total environ-
ment of the measured, insofar as what is measured and thus placed

into a determinate setting *is* so by virtue of its relation to
purpose. Thus the phenomenon of depth seems to involve an
irreducible transcendence, in the rudimentary sense of surpassing
what is fixed, measured, determinate.

What we now wish to propose is that the experience of one
or more of the several steps involved in the journey toward
depth is an experience, however evasive and infrequent, which is
very much an important element in our current, secular experience
of the world. We may indeed understand ourselves predominately
in terms of the task of world-appropriation and world-involvement,
but the evanescent lapses into depth also indicates to us that
the world, i.e., the overall context of relatedness which determines the meaning of human being, itself must encompass more than
surface involvement founded in projected purpose. The world is
more than our usual pattern of involvements, and consequently
more than the things and persons which fit into those involvements, because it also includes the phenomenon of depth. We
therefore do not need to move beyond the world in the sense of
a reality separated from the world by its utter self-consummation
in order to discern a real need for raising the question of
transcendence.

What we would now like to propose is that this question can
and should be raised on the twofold basis of first, the root
meaning of the word itself, and second, the evanescent occurrence
within human life of the phenomenon of depth. Our inquiry into
the meaning of transcendence is thus to be guided by the following set of questions: 1) Is it meaningful to speak of transcendence if transcendence is the surpassing found in the phenomenon
of depth? Is not this surpassing a passing beyond the realm of
significance and hence of meaning? Or is meaning somehow more
than significance, and if so, what does meaning itself mean?
2) How is it possible to think transcendence as in any sense
real, ultimate, or of irreducible importance in itself? Can it
be said that transcendence involves a movement beyond reality
itself? Is there an ontological thinking that is broad enough
to allow room for transcendence if transcendence takes us beyond
the realm of reality itself (in the sense of the actual, that
which is given to present itself to us)? 3) How is it possible
to encounter transcendence, and what does such encounter mean

for human life? Does such encounter address human ill-being,
and if so does it amount to the source of salvation? Can one
speak of salvation any more in this connection? 4) And finally,
how does this inquiry into the meaning of transcendence relate
to the question of God?

Prolepsis of the Ensuing Work

Because our inquiry into transcendence falls under the
rubric of "meaning," Chapter II will pursue at length an interpretation of meaning which is based largely upon the writings of
Hans Georg Gadamer. And in the course of this chapter, it will
be claimed that meaning as such is of a transcendent character
itself, and indeed in two senses: First, meaning will be shown
to be transcendent with respect to consciousness and hence human
subjectivity. And second, meaning will be shown to be transcendent with respect to the appearance of all particular things,
what we customarily term "the objective." In both of these
cases, the transcendence of meaning is to be understood as a
surpassing in the sense of *ontological primacy*. Meaning has the
primacy both with respect to consciousness and with respect to
the appearance, the particular coming-forth of things. As such,
meaning surpasses the structural parameters of both subjectivity
and objectivity. Meaning can thus be understood within neither
of these so-called regions of being but must rather be interpreted anew on its own terms, and as it gives itself to be
interpreted.

There is an obvious circularity present in this movement
from the inquiry into the meaning of transcendence to the claim
of the transcendence of meaning. And it is because of this
circularity that we cannot demonstrate ahead of time the justification for pursuing transcendence in terms of the essence of
meaning. However, the outcome of our inquiry into meaning as
such should confirm the starting point, especially if meaning as
such is itself found to be transcendent in character. We raise
the question of the *meaning* of transcendence as such because in
the end we will uncover the *transcendence* of meaning.

The turn from the question of the *meaning* of transcendence
to the discovery of the *transcendence* of meaning, raises the

question of how it is possible to think the transcendence of
meaning. Chapter III will attempt to address this question by
presenting a global understanding of being and human being which
is based upon the life-long work of Martin Heidegger. In this
global understanding a way of thinking comes to the fore in
which the transcendence of meaning is thinkable in terms of the
primordial relatedness of being as such and human being.

Having presented the global context for our thinking concerning the transcendence of meaning, we will then proceed in
Chapter IV to explore the special way in which transcendence
gives itself to be understood. In order to do this, we will
appeal to the understanding of meaning as a fourfold regioning
that is suggested in some of Heidegger's later writings. At
this time, we will discover that one of the interplaying domains
of the fourfold meaning is the Holy, that meaning-domain which
can be characterized as 1) the "place" of overwhelming claim
(divinity), and 2) utter noncircumventability. With the
discussion of the Holy, we will have arrived at the "place" at
which the meaning of transcendence as such emerges as the transcendence of meaning.

Following this (still in Chapter IV), we will discuss
Heidegger's attempt to give thought to the destiny of being. In
particular, we will consider his claim that the destiny of being
is now culminating in a pervasive "climate" of meaning which
Heidegger terms *Ge-Stell* and which we translate as "gathering-
into-orderability." This discussion of gathering-into-orderability is relevant to our purpose for the following reason. Gathering-into-orderability, as the gathering of all that appears into
availability for calculation, use, management, poses a fundamental
danger to the fourfold of meaning and hence to the Holy, the
domain of the self-giving of meaning as transcendence. Heidegger's
claim in this connection seems to be that the Holy as an "aspect"
of the fourfold of meaning is itself darkened under the prevalence
of gathering-into-orderability, such that for the most part at
least, the divinity which emerges in the Holy is no longer plac-
ing human being under its claim. To the extent that this darkening or closing-up of the Holy now prevails, one is left only
with the afterimage of the transcendence of meaning, that is,
with the *absence* of divinity. But in Heidegger's thinking, the

rule of gathering-into-orderability is not absolute. Despite
its rarity, there may transpire the "flashing" of the full context of meaning, such that the Holy and the self-giving of
meaning as transcendence which is encountered there, may yet be
experienced. This flashing and its characterization as "bringing-into-ownness" will occupy the remainder of Chapter IV.

In conclusion, Chapter V will pursue the theological consequences of our inquiry into the meaning of transcendence as such.
These consequences will include the theological claim that even
though the absence of divinity must in one sense be affirmed,
nevertheless when the Holy flashes, one is taken beyond mere
absence into pure mystery. In addition, mystery will be characterized (although certainly not in categoreal fashion) as the
pervasive mutuality that brings all things into primordial
belongingness. And finally, some implications of the meaning of
transcendence as the primordial claim upon human being of the
mystery of mutuality, ownness, for the use of the term "God"
will be suggested.

CHAPTER II

THE ONTOLOGICAL IMPORT OF MEANING

The purpose of this chapter is to provide an interpretation
of meaning, in line with our overall attempt to think the meaning of transcendence as such. And as we have already indicated,
this chapter will maintain that transcendence as such characterizes all meaning, such that the meaning of transcendence is to
be discerned in the transcendence of meaning.

How, then, does one go about the business of interpreting
meaning as meaning, or the essence of meaning? In order to do
this, one must turn one's attention to language. After all,
language is clearly the medium of meaning. It is the medium in
which meaning resides and through which it is brought to bear
upon our lives, our experience, our understanding. To investigate the essence of meaning must therefore involve the task of
investigating the essence of language.

In what follows, we will first consider one rather prominent interpretation of the essence of language and meaning which
stems from Plato and culminates in the view of the early
Wittgenstein that the essence of meaning is *signification*. In
its simplest guise this view holds that words, and accordingly
language itself, function as names or designations of pre-given
realities and/or states of affairs. In contrast to this view,
we will then present the interpretation of Hans Georg Gadamer
who accords to meaning and to language as the indispensable
medium of meaning a strict priority relative to what is definitely and concretely given in experience. We will find ourselves
in agreement with this latter view, and will expand it in the
direction laid out by our concern for the meaning of transcendence.

Meaning and Signification

The first step to be taken in our consideration of the
nature of meaning is to consider the rather prevalent view that
meaning is signification. The clearest and most consistent
presentation of this view is to be found in Ludwig Wittgenstein's

Tractatus Logico-Philosophicus.[1] Accordingly, it may be useful
to look briefly at the claims regarding language and meaning
proffered by this work, in order to have before us a clear and
consistent interpretation of the essence of meaning as signification.

To be sure, it is true that Wittgenstein himself left this
early work behind in the later stages of his philosophical
development. And part of the shift in his thinking is to be
seen in his later emphasis upon the need for a descriptive
inquiry into the many ways that language can in fact be seen to
perform. This later attitude toward meaning and language can
be encapsulated in the formula: meaning is however language is
used.[2] But it is still useful and enlightening to go back to
the *Tractatus*, because it is in this work that certain fundamental
presuppositions concerning the relation of language and meaning
to the world and reality are laid totally bare. And since these
presuppositions may still be governing much of our thinking concerning what is most basically true, this early work of Wittgenstein can serve very well to set the stage for the alternative
understanding of meaning, language and world that we find in
Gadamer's work.

The theory of meaning underlying the *Tractatus* is that the
essence of meaning is signification. In its simplest form,
signification is the naming function of a simple word unambiguously designating a simple object (prop. 3.202). In this case, the
name means solely and precisely insofar as it signifies a single
object. It follows, then, that the object itself *is* the meaning
of the name (prop. 3.203). But names do not mean except as they
occur in propositions. Hence, meaning is properly seen as
propositional (prop. 3.3). Now the proposition itself is also a
sign, in that it pictures the structure of possible fact (props.
3.12, 3.32, 4.021). Meaning in its proper sense is thus more
complex than the simple naming function; meaning is rather the
picturing function of the proposition in relation to some
possible fact or state of affairs. Thus, the meaning of a
proposition is the possible fact or state of affairs that is
pictured by it (props. 4.03-4.0311).

An interesting feature of this theory should now be noted.
Ideally, so to speak, the meaning of a proposition is that actual

fact or state of affairs which the proposition pictures or
mirrors in a direct, structural correspondence (props. 2.15,
2.1514). However, this formulation applies only to *true* (correct) propositions. False (incorrect) propositions cannot be
meaningful in the strict terms of this formulation. Therefore,
it must be said that the meaning of the propositional sign is
the *possible* state of affairs which the proposition pictures, not
the *actual* state of affairs (props. 2.2-2.222, 3.13). Truth and
falsity are accordingly understood, not as properties of the
proposition, but as the agreement or disagreement of the propositional picture with actual fact (props. 2.222, 4.06-4.063, 6.111).
Furthermore, language is understood as the totality of propositions (prop. 4.001). Hence, language functions by representing
possible fact, and is unable to transcend this function without
becoming meaningless in a strict sense (props. 4.12, 6.54).

This is the kernel of the theory of meaning and language as
presented in the *Tractatus*. But the implications which Wittgenstein draws from this theory are equally instructive. In his
thoroughgoing consistency he discovers that such traditional
areas of purported meaning as ethics, metaphysics and religion
are strictly speaking quite meaningless in that the propositions
that are advanced in these fields cannot possibly picture any
factual state (props. 6.4-6.53). To be sure, this does not stop
Wittgenstein from speaking of the mystical (a feeling), or of
ethics and aesthetics as "transcendental" (props. 6.44-6.45,
6.421). It has, of course, been frequently suggested that
Wittgenstein's refusal simply to repudiate these technically
meaningless realms already points to his later, descriptive
approach to the various ways that language is used. Nevertheless,
his judgment that ethics, metaphysics and religion are strictly
meaningless does follow from the basic premise that meaning is
signification, given that the sign functions to indicate some
possible state of affairs, or if one can so speak, some possible
actuality.

It is now time to note some of the underlying presuppositions
that coalesce in this view. The most important of these is the
primacy accorded to actuality, to given fact. As we have seen,
meaning is utterly subordinated to the factual, even to the
point of identifying meaning with propositional representation

of actuality, or more strictly, with purported actuality. This primacy accorded to actual fact is shown to be presupposed in the *Tractatus* by its very first proposition, which simply states this assumption: "The world is everything that is the case." Given this presupposition, meaning must then be subordinated to actuality; meaning must be viewed as the representation of the sheer appearance of whatever is, or of what might possibly appear in factual givenness.

The primary reason for turning our attention to the *Tractatus* is our view that this work best allows certain fundamental and pervasive presuppositions to come to light, presuppositions whose sway may extend far beyond the actual, explicit position that is advanced there. We have now isolated one of these presuppositions, namely, that what is actual is more fundamental than what is non-actual or other than actual. And indeed, is this not a pervasive presupposition of our ordinary way of thinking? If we can understand the actual as anything whatever that can enter into some mode of self-identical appearance, then it would seem that we, as a matter of course, do accord to actuality the privileged position of primary rank in the order of being. Furthermore, we tend to interpret the meaning of being itself as the pervasive holding-sway of actuality or self-identical appearance. This presupposition of the primacy of actuality thus has a much wider sphere of influence than that defined by adherence to the elaborated position of the *Tractatus*.

There are several other presuppositions that come to light in the *Tractatus*, each of which is closely related to the presupposition of the primacy of actual fact. One of these additional presuppositions is that the negative has no real place within the world as a whole. In other words, this presupposition is a denial of negativity, a rejection of negativity as an independent element of importance. This denial is also given explicit expression in the *Tractatus*:

> That, however, the signs "p" and "-p" *can* say the same thing is important, for it shows that the sign "-" corresponds to nothing in reality.
> That negation occurs in a proposition, is no characteristic of its sense (--p=p).
> The propositions "p" and "-p" have opposite senses, but to them corresponds one and the same reality. (prop. 4.0621)

It is interesting to note that what this passage expresses is
not itself a representation of actual fact, but rather a presupposition, even a prescription, that all that is thoughtworthy
and meaningful, all that bears on human life, *must* be predelin-
eated as positive fact and only as positive fact. The positive
is presumptively accorded fundamental and sovereign status.
Hence, the non-positive, those "meaning-spaces" which do not
sustain determinate givenness but are instead areas of indeterminacy, absence, emptiness, or perhaps the non-actual expansiveness
of undefined hope and promise, these non-positive "meaning-
spaces" are here denied to be of any importance in the make-up
of the total human world, and hence are simply dismissed and
ignored.

Again, we wish to suggest that this presupposition has a
sway that far outstretches the confines of the position taken up
in the *Tractatus*. Is it not the case that humans share an in-
grained predisposition to attend to the actual, to be taken by
it, to the point that one's concern and attention are fully
captured by the exigencies of actual fact? Is it not also the
case that we systematically ignore the lurking sway of the non-
actual, dismissing these regions of awareness as mere mood,
fantasy, inattention, absent-mindedness, depression, or the like?
To the extent that we find ourselves drawn into the factual as
that which seems to lie at the ground of importance, we also fall
under the dominion of the rule of the positive.

A third and final presupposition that we will lift out of
the pages of the *Tractatus* is the presumption that possibility
has no genuine status of its own, but is merely the refraction
of what actually is, and as such is utterly dependent on such
actuality. In the view of the *Tractatus*, possibility does seem
to show up in the proposition inasmuch as the proposition represents a *possible* state of affairs. However, in the final analysis, the proposition is always either true or false. These two
are mutually exclusive and completely exhaustive alternatives.
Therefore, there is no possibility in its own right, for possibility must ultimately devolve either into the true or into the
false. The realm of the possible can have no genuine standing
in the world, for possibility is merely the illusory state in
which the question of truth (correct representation of fact) and

falsehood (incorrect representation of fact) has yet to be
resolved.

Given this denial that possibility genuinely enters on its
own into the essential make-up of the world, experiences of
hope, promise, an open future, etc., are either dismissed as
"unreal" or confined to the merely subjective realm of fantasy,
wish, or counter-factual desire. The world is simply all that
is the case, and is not inclusive of the indetermination of
possibility. There is thus literally no essential room for
possibility. One must simply live with what there is in actual
givenness, and consign possibility to the subordinate and arid
logical category that encompasses both factual and counter-
factual states of affairs.

Once again, we view this presupposition as outstripping the
Tractatus proper. Is it not correct to say that we are predis-
posed to attend to actuality, such that in the presence of the
actual, we experience the possible as illusory, unreal, unimpor-
tant? Do we not think of the actual as the "fulfillment" of the
possible, and thereby consign possibility to the utterly dependent status of "to-be-fulfilled-by-actuality"? If this is the
case, then this presupposition also characterizes our usual and
customary manner of interpreting our relatedness to the world,
which means that this presupposition is of far greater import
than the specific influence of Wittgenstein's early work.

As we have said, we directed our attention to the *Tractatus*
simply as a convenient way of bringing to light certain fundamental presuppositions of our pervasive manner of being in and
understanding the world. And we have focused on three such
presuppositions, namely, the primacy of the actual, the denial
of negativity as such, and the denial of possibility as such.
But in addition, we have hinted that these presuppositions are
inseparably interconnected with the interpretation of meaning
which holds its essence to be signification. Accordingly, in
our view it is not enough to point out the inadequacies of the
explicit theory of meaning as signification which is presented
in the *Tractatus*. More importantly, one needs to address the
presuppositions that underlie this theory, and consider whether
or not they should continue to go unchallenged.

It is now our intention to attempt to elucidate an

interpretation of meaning which challenges these presuppositions.
This challenge must occur and be sustained in the course of this
work, if we are to succeed in giving thought to the meaning of
transcendence as such. The presuppositions which we have isolated, each singly and taken together, would preclude any talk
of the meaning of transcendence. We have seen that the word
"transcendence" says "surpassing fixed limit, measure, determination." But the actual is precisely the arena of delimitation,
measure, determination. Accordingly, if transcendence is to have
any meaning on its own terms, and not simply as an abstract and
empty concept of otherness, there must be a genuine sense in
which meaning is not wedded to the primacy of the actual, nor
ultimately interpreted in terms of the actual. The presuppositions discussed above are, we believe, the bedrock expressions of
our predisposition toward the actual, and the primacy that is
automatically accorded it. Our interpretation of meaning, as
contrasting with the interpretation of meaning as signification,
must be radical enough to overcome the assumed primacy of the
actual in relation to meaning if our attempt to think the meaning
of transcendence on its own essential terms is to have any
chance of succeeding. With this in mind, we may now turn to
Gadamer's discussion of meaning and language, and ultimately to
his radical challenge to the interpretation of the essence of
meaning as signification.

Gadamer's Interpretation of Meaning and Language: Introduction

The heart of Gadamer's alternative to the view sketched
above lies in his claim that neither language nor meaning are
disjoined from the world, but rather are rudimentary constituents
of the world. In order to see what Gadamer means by this claim,
we might profit by a brief look at how he characterizes the
opposing view that language merely signifies the world without
being an essential constituent of it. Unlike Wittgenstein, who
saw the essence of the sign (and hence language) in its picturing
function, thus as itself a fact which replicates other facts in
a strictly univocal structural correspondence, Gadamer seems the
essence of the sign in its function of pointing away from itself
to something else. The sign is a sign precisely when it does not

draw attention to itself, as does a picture, but when it draws
attention to something other than itself, which it is intended
to indicate.

> For a sign is nothing but what its function demands;
> and that is, to point away from itself. In order to
> be able to fulfill this function, of course, it must
> first draw attention to itself. It must be striking:
> that is, it must be clearly defined and present itself
> as an indicator, like a poster. But neither a sign
> nor a poster is a picture. It should not attract
> attention to itself in a way that would cause one to
> linger over it, for it is there only to make present
> something that is not present, and in such a way that
> the thing that is not present is the only thing that
> is expressed.3

But even though Gadamer and the *Tractatus* disagree over the
nature of the sign (picture vs. indicator), they do agree that
the sign is *essentially other* than what it signifies or expresses.
This entails that that to which the sign points is itself non-
significatory (at least in relation to the sign which designates
it), although it is indeed the *terminus ad quem* of the signification.

This disjunction of the sign, with its significatory function, from the non-significatory object of the signification,
has had fateful consequences when used as the model for understanding how language means. When the way that language means
is understood to be signification, a disjunction is entailed
between language and the world. Gadamer himself traces this
disjunction back to Plato's *Cratylus*, in which names are found
not to be images or copies, with the result that the "true being
of things" is to be apprehended without regard to the names of
these things.4 The consequence of this disjunction of words
from the "true being of things" has, according to Gadamer,
fundamentally determined subsequent thought concerning the
nature of language.

> That the true being of things is to be investigated
> "without names" means that there is no access to
> truth in the proper being of words as such--even if
> all the investigation, questioning, answering,
> instructing and differentiation cannot of course take
> place without the help of language. This is to say
> that thought is so independent of the proper being
> of words, which it takes as mere signs through which
> what is referred to, the thought, the matter-for-
> thought, is brought into view, that the word adopts
> a wholly secondary relation to the matter-for-thought.5

Western thought concerning language accordingly has assumed
that language has nothing to do with being, but is rather a mere
instrument or tool through which being is referred to.

The non-linguisticality of the true being of things is,
indeed, the governing presupposition of the *Cratylus*. In this
work, which Gadamer describes as the fundamental statement of
Greek thought on language, two opposing theories of the relation
of language and being are discussed. One of the theories,
espoused by Hermogenes, maintains that the relation of a word
to the object which it names is merely conventional, such that
the meaning of a word derives solely from agreed-upon usage.[6]
In this view, there is no relation other than conventional agreement which binds the word to that which it names. Socrates
responds to Hermogenes, first, by maintaining that things must
have "their own proper and permanent essence," in order for
there to be any distinction between truth and error, knowledge
and ignorance.[7] But words (names) are instruments for distin-
guishing things according to their natures.[8] Hence Socrates
concludes that there must be proper (correct) and improper
(incorrect) names, since the distinctive essence of a thing
entails a name which is correctly used to distinguish the thing
named from other things according to their differing, permanent
natures.[9]

The other theory discussed in the *Cratylus* is one espoused
by Cratylus himself. This theory lies at the opposing extreme
from that argued by Hermogenes, for it claims that to be a name,
and not a mere clamoring sound, means to present the true being
of a thing by imitating it in some way.[10] In this view, words
are not only like the things which they name, but they are the
means whereby knowledge of the thing is attained.[11] Words are
thus treated as parts of nature, such that by nature, there is
a "right" name for each thing.

At first glance, this theory seems to be a mere extension
of Socrates' findings in his discussion with Hermogenes. However, as Socrates proceeds to clarify Cratylus' position, he
reveals it to be as untenable as Hermogenes' original opinion.

This clarification begins with a distinction between primary
and secondary names, primary names being those which can no
longer be analyzed into parts which are themselves still names.[12]

Socrates then proceeds to identify primary names with letters
and syllables, primarily letters.[13] The question then arises as
to how primary names (letters) serve to represent the true nature
of things. If this can be answered, then presumably the way in
which larger linguistic units serve to imitate the true natures
of things can also be understood as a compound form of the
simplest imitation of the thing by the letter.[14] The nature of
simple imitation is then taken by Socrates not to be exact
duplication, but rather to be the image which does not reproduce
every feature of the original, but merely represents in some
way the "general character of the thing."[15]

The weakness of this view first begins to become apparent
when Socrates points out that as a matter of fact, letters
simply do not occur as primary images of things, nor of the
fundamental elements and features that comprise things.[16] But
the decisive blow to this theory comes when Socrates suggests
that the "naturalness" or rightness of a name can be verified
only if one compares the name with the thing itself. Otherwise,
no sense can be made of the name as a representative image of
the thing. This problem becomes even more acute when it is
recognized that words seem to conflict with each other in their
representations of things. How is this conflict to be resolved
except by recourse to some direct knowledge of things themselves
that is not mediated through names?[17] The conclusion seems
inevitable that either there is no such thing as truth, or that
truth is to be found by means of thought which is not bound to
language. Thus, Socrates concludes that true being is to be
investigated independently of the meanings of words, and hence
in independence of language:

> How real existence is to be studied or discovered is,
> I suspect, beyond you and me. But we may admit so
> much, that the knowledge of things is not to be
> derived from names. No, they must be studied and
> investigated in themselves.[18]

An important outgrowth of this Platonic view of the non-
linguisticality of true being should now be noted. Given that
there must be a more direct knowledge of things than any knowledge
supplied through the meanings of words, the way is left open for
meaning itself to be divorced from language. That there may
not be any permanent, self-subsistent meanings to things is

certainly not the implication that Plato draws from the cognitive inadequacy of linguistic meanings. Rather the permanent,
self-subsistent meanings (natures) of things are to be discovered
in pure thought (*noein*) which directly perceives the essential
being of things without recourse to words. Accordingly, Plato
states in his *Seventh Letter* that "no intelligent man will ever
be so bold as to put into language those things which his reason
has contemplated."[19] Thought is thus divorced from language;
thought becomes the pure apprehension of the abiding Ideas, and
language is seen as a secondary *tool* of thought which certainly
has pragmatic utility for instruction and communication, but is
not of primary importance where knowledge is concerned. To be
sure, the difficulties which Socrates found in the pure conven-
tionalist theory of Hermogenes indicates that Plato did allow
for some principle of similarity to operate between words and
things, but not one that is of any primary cognitive significance.
Thus Gadamer concludes:

> The convention which is present in the practical use
> of language and which alone comprises the rightness
> of words may possibly make use of the principle of
> similarity, but it is not bound to do so. This is a
> very moderate position, but one which includes the
> fundamental presupposition that words have no real
> cognitive significance--a result which points beyond
> the entire sphere of words and the question of their
> rightness to the knowledge of the subject-matter
> (*Sache*). Obviously such knowledge is what alone
> matters to Plato.[20]

It is thus not unfair to view the *Cratylus* as preparing the
way for the following, decisive results which have been determin-
ative for the subsequent philosophy of language. The divorce
of meaning from language established meaning as the abiding
structure of pure possibility, a structure made up of those
universal determinants of thought and being which together comprise a domain of pure, intelligible presence. In the English
philosophical tradition, this result has been most fully inherited in our century by Alfred North Whitehead. In Whitehead's
thought, this inheritance is seen clearly in the distinction
that he draws between the primordial and the consequent natures
of God. It is certainly true that Whitehead conceives the ultimate characteristic of being to be "creativity," that is, the
universal process in which the disjunctively given elements of

the immediate past become the conjunctive unity of an actual
occasion of subjective experience.[21] However, the outcome of
creativity is in every case subject to the relevant possibilities
that are finally derived from a primordial conceptual valuation
of the entire realm of pure potentiality.[22] Thus we have the
ground of all determinate actuality located in a realm of self-
subsistent, abiding, non-linguistic meaning.

This primordial conceptual valuation of the pure possibilities of being (the pure, abiding *meaning* of being) is itself, to
be sure, "deficiently actual," and hence is essentially an
abstraction from the full reality of God which emerges in the
ongoing divine prehension of the successive phases of the world-
process (i.e., God's consequent nature).[23] Nevertheless, the
primordial conceptual valuation is itself not subject to that
process, but rather constitutes a primordial sphere of essential,
self-same presence, regardless of its lack of independence. As
Whitehead says, "God's conceptual nature is unchanged, by reason
of its final completedness."[24] Thus, for Whitehead, the meaning
of being is construed in terms of intelligible, abiding presence,
a presence which is directly grasped by pure thought. Here, as
with Plato, meaning is divorced from language and is taken to
be a structure of pure possibility which, when seen in relation
to the human world and the "occasional" character of communication through language, is itself a realm apart, abiding in
itself.

It must be recognized that Plato's investigation of language
and meaning in the *Cratylus* begins with the presupposition that
the meaning of true being must be self-same and abiding, i.e.,
must be conceived in terms of pure, intelligible presence. From
the outset, the question of the truth of language is conceived
as a question concerning the relation of the word to the original,
non-occasional nature of the thing. Hence, the truth of language
has to be considered in terms of the correctness or rightness of
words: do the words which name things correctly represent the
original things which they name? Or, on the other hand, does
correct representation make any sense as a criterion or an ideal
when applied to mere words? This is the frame within which the
question of the nature of linguistic meaning is raised in the
Cratylus; linguistic meaning is already seen in relation to the

more primary sphere or level of pure presence. Consequently,
the *Cratylus* marks the beginning of the ongoing failure of
Western thought to question linguistic meaning from its own
center.

Given this limitation of the way in which the question of
linguistic meaning is itself raised, it is a relatively easy
thing for Socrates to reduce to absurdity the theory that words
actually do serve as correct images of things, as representations
of the essential natures (meanings) of things. The convention-
alist theory is thus the real winner of the discussion in the
Cratylus. Words do not mean by serving as correct images of
pre-given things--this Socrates easily shows. Therefore, words
must have their essential being in mere signification, that is,
in a conventional sign-function. Words are thus objects whose
being is exhausted in an associative function; they are mere
instruments whose ability to signify has nothing whatever to do
with their own proper content, or with their own proper occurrence. This is the result for the subsequent Western understanding of language which Gadamer sees to derive from the *Cratylus*.
The outcome of this, of course, is the rise of the notion of a
purely unambiguous, strictly conventional ideal language, whose
unambiguously defined symbols would correspond exactly to the
totality of absolutely available objects.[25] Thus, in Plato's
Cratylus are already sown the seeds which finally flower, among
other places, in the ideal language theory of Wittgenstein's
Tractatus.

This development, stemming from the *Cratylus* and reaching
a culmination of sorts in the *Tractatus*, stands in stark contrast
to Gadamer's attempt to understand the being of language. As
we have previously noted, Gadamer rejects any disjunction of
language, meaning and world. On the contrary, the interinvolvement of these three comprises a unity, a unity which is itself
the event of understanding that founds human being-in-the-world.
The task now at hand is to explicate and to defend this proposal.

The basis for Gadamer's rejection of the tendency of thought
initiated by the *Cratylus* is the latter's unfounded presupposition that words, i.e., names, are the primordial exemplification
of the linguistic. In contrast to this presupposition, Gadamer
argues that:

> In all this [i.e., in the entire discussion between
> Socrates and Cratylus], however, it is not recognized
> that the truth of things (*Sachen*) is situated in
> speech, which is to say ultimately in the intending
> (*Meinen*) of a unified meaning (*Meinung*) concerning
> things, and not in the individual words--also not
> in the entire stock of words of a language.26

The starting point for understanding Gadamer's interpretation
of meaning and language is thus the claim that the conveyance
of meaning by language is not an atomistic function of individual
words, construed inevitably as names of things which are essentially other than and prior to words, but is rather *what occurs
in the whole of language*, such that individual expressions and
words convey meaning only as parts which reflect the whole of
a totality of meaning.

The notion that Gadamer uses in this context to express the
way that language conveys meaning is the difficult notion of
speculation. Language conveys meaning, not through a dispensa-
tion into univocal sign-functions, but through a kind of infinitely open-ended mirroring in which the definite sense-possibili-
ties of a word or expression reflect an unexpressed infinity of
meaning.27 Herein lies the heart of Gadamer's philosophy of
meaning and language, and accordingly we will need to pay special
attention to the claim that is here advanced. At the outset we
can say that the "infinity of meaning" here spoken of is not
construed, as in Whitehead (or Plato for that matter), to be a
primordial, timeless sphere of pure intelligible presence, a
given totality of possibilities that abide as intelligible self-
sameness in a standing relational structure. Gadamer's "infinity
of meaning" is not to be understood as intelligible presence.
And because it is not so understood, the meaning of any linguistic
expression can never be fulfilled eidetically, nor by implication
can it ever be exhausted by any set of strictly univocal, exact
representations. Language in essence is neither univocal nor
exact.28 Instead, it is more like the occurrence of open-ended
reflection, which brings with it a kind of inexhaustibility,
the infinite possibility of further reflection into new contexts
and circumstances.

The Speculative Unity of Meaning and World

What, then, does Gadamer intend when he uses the notion of
"speculation" to characterize the essence of language? In
employing this term, Gadamer means to refer to the mirror relation, to the mysterious way that the reflecting medium *both is
the same as, yet is more than* the appearance of what is reflected.

> The word "speculative" here refers to the mirror
> relation. Being reflected involves a constant
> substitution. When something is reflected in some-
> thing else, say, the castle in the lake, it means
> that the lake throws back the image of the castle.
> The mirror image is essentially connected, through
> the medium of the observer, with the proper vision
> of the thing. It has no being of its own, it is
> like an "appearance" which is not itself and yet
> allows the proper vision to appear as a mirror image.
> It is like a duplication, which yet exists as only
> one thing. The real mystery of reflection is precisely
> the ungraspability of the picture, the free-floating
> character of pure reproduction.[29]

What needs to be noted in this passage is that the reflection
cannot be grasped as anything different from that which is
reflected, and yet it is somehow additional to the latter. The
reflection has a unity of being with what is reflected, yet such
that the reflection is also more; it is a *presentation* that does
not simply reside in the appearance of what is presented, for it
is also manifest as a duplication. In this way, the presentation
that occurs in reflection reveals an infinite possibility for
further reflection, further presentation *of the same.*

These points can be further elaborated in terms of Gadamer's
own example of reflection, namely, the castle reflected in the
lake. Obviously, an observer of such a scene must acknowledge
that the reflection of the castle in the lake is in addition to
the presence of the castle up on the hill overlooking the lake.
The reflected appearance of the castle is more than the presence
of the castle on the hill. But is it different? Or is it the
same?

If, instead of taking in the entire scene, the observer
peers solely into the lake, that is, into the reflection of the
castle, what does he find there? In truth, what he finds is
nothing but an appearance of the castle itself. Taken on its
own terms, the reflection is every bit an original presentation

of the castle, the castle itself brought into an original appearance. What is present as the castle on the hill and the castle
reflected in the lake is the *same*.

   To be sure, if the observer again withdraws his gaze from
its absorption in the lake's reflection, and attends to the
castle on the hill overlooking the lake, he must then admit that
the reflected castle is a duplication of the castle on the hill.
Indeed he must, but does this admission somehow impugn the
appearance of the castle in the lake, or in any way destroy the
presentative power of the lake as a reflecting medium? To
answer this, the observer need only look once again into the
lake, and he still will find *the castle itself* brought fully into
an appearance of itself. He will not find a representation of
the castle, or a copy of the castle, but rather a genuine
appearance of the castle.

   This distinction between appearance and copy is central to
the understanding of the mirror-relation as a metaphor for the
speculative character of language. Consequently, we must consider just why a reflected appearance is said to be essentially
different from a copy. Concerning the nature of a copy, Gadamer
has this to say:

> It lies in the essence of the copy that it has no
> other task but to resemble the original. The measure
> of its adequacy is that one is able to recognize the
> original in the copy. This means that it is so deter-
> mined that it gives up its own being-for-itself [*sein
> eigenes Fürsich-sein aufzuheben*] so as to serve
> completely the mediation of that which is copied....
> The copy gives itself up in the sense that it functions
> as a means, and like all means loses its function in
> the achievement of its goal. It is for-itself simply
> in order to give itself up. This giving-up-of-itself
> is an intentional element in the being of the copy
> itself.30

On the basis of this characterization of the essence of the copy,
we can now see why it is incorrect to interpret reflective
appearance as a manner of copying. As is said in the above
passage, the copy exists in order to abandon its own being in
favor of the original. In its essence, the copy distinguishes
its own being from the original, and totally subordinates its
being to that of the original. But reflective appearance does
not in itself make any such distinction between its being and

the being of an original. If one allows reflected appearance
to occur on its own terms, without superimposing upon it evalua-
tive criteria brought in from outside, one discovers that *as*
appearance, reflection is as primary as other modes of appearance. In the case of the reflected castle, this occurs not as
a secondary copy essentially dependent upon an original, but
taken on its own terms (i.e., where comparison with the castle
overlooking the lake is not involved), it occurs simply as an
appearance of the castle itself. In this connection Gadamer
says:

> The ideal copy would therefore seem to be the mirror-
> image [*Spiegelbild*], for its being is actually such
> as to disappear. It occurs only for the one who
> looks into the mirror, and beyond its pure appearance
> it is nothing. In truth, however, the mirror-image
> is neither a picture [*Bild*] nor a copy [*Abbild*], for
> it has no being-for-itself. The mirror throws back
> the image [*Bild*], that is to say, the mirror makes
> visible to someone what it mirrors only so long as
> one looks into the mirror and perceives his own
> image therein, or whatever else is mirrored in it.
> It is no accident that we speak here of image [*Bild*]
> and not of a copy or illustration. For in the mirror-
> image, things [*das Seiende*] themselves appear in the
> image so that I have the thing itself in the mirror-
> image.[31]

The central claim here is that when taken on its own terms, the
reflected image has no being of its own which is something
additional to the being of what is reflected. There is a unity
of being between the reflected appearance of the castle, and
the presence of the castle on the hill. These two are *the same*.

It is also true to say that the reflected appearance is
a duplication, and hence is not strictly *identical* to the presence of the castle on the hill. In the reflection, something
additional takes place. The presence of the castle is happening
in excess of its non-reflected appearance up on the hill. And
yet, it is still the castle itself that is present in this
excess. What is the same, the presence of the castle, is also
different, in that the reflected appearance is additional to
the non-reflected appearance.

The paradox that what is the same is also different points
into the heart of the mystery of reflection. It is not enough
to say that the mirrored appearance has no additional being of

its own, and is thus the same as what is reflected. One must
add to this that mirror-reflection injects into the sameness
of something's self-showing an infinite open-endedness that
finally must subvert any attempt to understand the sameness of
what appears in reflection in terms of simple, self-coincident
identity. The duplication inherent in reflection reveals that
the being of the castle is not self-contained in its non-
mirrored appearance up on the hill overlooking the lake, but is
rather an open-ended availability for further coming-into-appearance. Its being must be understood as such an availability
rather than as finite, self-identical presence if the mirror-
reflection of the castle is unified in being with the non-
reflected presence of the castle. The being of the castle is
therefore not restricted to a single, *finite* appearance, but in
reflection is revealed to be the possibility of infinitely
duplicated appearance, or an infinitely open-ended horizon of
appearance. Mirror-reflection, thus, is both the same as the
finite appearance which it sustains, and is also *more* than such
finite appearance, in that it is an infinitely extended "power"
of additional coming-into-appearance.

    We must now attempt to apply this metaphor of reflection
in a mirror to language, and through this metaphor to illuminate
the speculative essence of language. We will begin with the
speculative unity which language exhibits, and then in a later
section we will consider the speculative "difference" which is
also revealed in the heart of language. To speak of speculative
unity in relation to language is to indicate a sameness between
linguistic expression and what is said in language. Just as in
the case of the mirror-image, language has no being-for-itself
that is other than what is said in language. Language is not
a means (a copy, a sign) that exhausts its being in the function
of bringing an original to recognition. On the contrary, the
being of language is precisely and simply the *appearance* of
whatever is said in it.

    But what does it mean to say that the appearance of what
is expressed in language is the same as language itself? It
means that such appearance is itself linguistic, and not pre-
linguistic. To put it another way, it means that there is no
such thing as an absolutely pure givenness which is only later

put into language after the fact. What appears never originally
appears as a simple surd, whose appearance is utterly discrete,
a sheer thereness. Instead, what appears always appears *as
something* first and foremost. And this "as something" means the
same as to say that appearance is originally linguistic, that
language and what is said in language are the same.

The analysis which discovered that original appearance is
always appearance as...is first worked out in Heidegger's *Sein
und Zeit*, section 33.[32] A brief consideration of this analysis
may prove helpful to us now in bringing to light what is here
meant by the unity of being between language and what is said
in language.

A common understanding of language is that language con-
sists of statements or assertions which attribute something to
a pre-given thing. If we start with this common understanding
of language, we are led to say that the appearance of things
is pre- or non-linguistic. Things simply are apparent, and
language comes along after whenever someone attributes something
(predicate, property, function, etc.) in an assertion to the
pre-given thing (subject). Language is thus a way of drawing
attention to, analyzing, and signifying what is already there
for such characterization.

Heidegger does not deny that *assertion* is a means of signifying what is pre-given (in his terminology, "present-at-hand"
[*vorhanden*]), but he does dispute the claim that language can
be understood on the basis of assertion. Indeed, if one
attempts to give a full account of assertion, one will discover
that assertion points beyond itself to the more fundamental
essence of the linguistic. To see this, one must attend to the
fact that assertion says something of something, and thus *describes* something *as* something. This "as" of assertion serves
to express a definite characteristic of something already given
relative to the act of assertion. However, the "as" of assertion, which Heidegger terms the "apophantic as," is possible
only on the ontological basis of a more primordial "as." We
can characterize something as something in a statement only
because the thing has *already* appeared as something, i.e., as
itself. In other words, unless something has already appeared
in a definite way and as already related in whatever fashion

to all other things within a global context of involvements, it
cannot be the subject of assertion. Things can be characterized
in assertion only because they already appear as something
definite within an overall context of meaningful interrelation
and interconnection. This primordial "as" which lies at the
base of the apophantic "as" of assertion Heidegger terms the
"existential-*hermeneutical* 'as'."[33]

Let us illustrate this distinction. To assert that a
bookcase is large, full of books, empty, broken, etc., is to
assert something of the bookcase and thus to describe the bookcase in some definite way as something or other. The bookcase
precedes the assertion of some characteristic of the bookcase.
This is the apophantic "as." But one could not characterize
the bookcase in this fashion unless the bookcase had already
appeared *as bookcase* (i.e., hermeneutically), that is, as a
physical object which is intended to hold books. This can be
expanded by considering that to appear as bookcase, the physical
object must already appear in meaningful relation to the entire
realm of being which is contained in books, i.e., the realm of
the written word, which includes all recorded information, all
theory, all poetry, all record of divine-human intercourse,
all recorded fantasy and speculation, etc. The bookcase appears
originally *as bookcase* only insofar as it occurs as the place
where books are held in readiness for consultation, and thus as
already bearing in its own being as bookcase a relatedness to
the entire realm of the written word. Thus, a bookcase appears
as bookcase only in an open context of involvement. The bookcase does not appear originally as a surd simply there, as a
sheerly self-contained, discrete entity, but rather it appears
as something, and this means that it appears as itself only
insofar as its appearance includes a global relatedness within
which and only within which it is itself.[34]

This fact, that the original appearance of something is
not sheer givenness but rather appearance within a global context of relatedness means that the thing gives itself *to be
understood*. The thing is present meaningfully, and can be
understood as something, only because it occurs in an open global context of involvement, i.e., a context of understanding,
and as already interrelated throughout that context.

If we return now to Gadamer, we can see in this discussion
of the way the bookcase appears an example of his claim that
the being of original appearance is itself linguistic. As he
says: "That which can be understood is language. This means
that it is such that it presents itself to be understood."[35]
Here, then, we encounter the claim that there is a unity between
language and what is said in language. The appearance of the
bookcase is what is said in language. But if its original
appearance is already hermeneutical, i.e., essentially exhibiting
a context of involvement within which it can meaningfully appear
as bookcase and not as mere surd, then the original appearance
is not pre-linguistic but rather linguistic in the sense of
"that which can be understood." Language is thus the same as
the appearance of what is expressed in language.

Moreover, this sameness must be understood to be ontological. As Gadamer says:

> To come to language does not mean that a second being
> [*Dasein*] is required. For something to present it-
> self as what it is belongs rather to its own being....
> What comes to language is not pre-given non-linguist-
> ically, but rather receives in the word its own
> determination [*Bestimmtheit*].[36]

If we go along with the claim expressed here that the being of
something is the way it appears, the way it presents itself,
then the being of something is linguistic, given that its appearance is linguistic. The bookcase gives itself to be understood
meaningfully, i.e., it gives itself as essentially related to
a global context of involvement. Its appearance is linguistic,
and so its being is also linguistic. Accordingly we say that
an ontological sameness obtains between language and what is
said in language.

At this point it is appropriate to see how the metaphor of
reflection in a mirror illuminates the sameness of being between
language and what is said in language. Seen in the light of
the mirror-metaphor, language does not re-present what is said
in language as a copy would, but instead language occurs as an
original presentation of what is said. Just as the reflected
castle is an original presentation of the castle itself, so also
language reflects what is said in language and thus occurs as
a primary coming-to-appearance. What is said in language is

thereby collected into appearance, and thus first presents itself *as* it is. And since the being of anything can be understood
as its presence, i.e., the manner of its genuine self-showing,
the being of what is said in language is speculatively the same
as language itself.

Several implications may be drawn from the speculative unity
of language and what is said in language. To begin with, this
unity entails that language is the proper site of meaning, and
furthermore its sole site. Meaning is always linguistic meaning. To show this, one must first realize that meaning is always
related to understanding as that which can be understood. Now,
everything that can be understood finds expression in language,
whether written or spoken, for as we have seen, the understandable appearance of something is already linguistic. Thus, the
unity of being between language and what is said in language
is itself meaning, the site of meaning's occurrence.

A second implication of the speculative unity obtaining
between language and what is said in language is that meaning
cannot be located in subjectivity, nor seen as a conscious overlay to something pre-given. If language is the same as what is
said in language, then the claim that all meaning is linguistic
does not imply that language is subjective, or merely a form of
consciousness. Instead, linguistic meaning is nothing other than
the speculative coming-forth of anything into understandability,
its genuine self-presentment as meaning, i.e., as something that
is related in a world-extensive context. Now surely it makes no
sense to interpret the genuine self-presentment of anything as
a subjective occurrence, for to do so obviates the distinction
between subjective and objective and thus is to no avail.
Accordingly, Gadamer has said:

> We have seen that words which express a subject-
> matter [*eine Sache*] are themselves seen to be a
> speculative occurrence. Their truth lies in what
> is said in them, and not in an opinion [*Meinen*]
> that is locked in the impotence of subjective
> particularity.[37]

Meaning is not subjective representation, but is rather *how* something comes speculatively into understandable appearance in
language.[38] Meaning is neither subjective (representation by
linguistic sign), nor objective (supra-linguistic form or eidos),

but is rather the unity of language and whatever it speculatively
presents.

A third implication of the speculative unity between language and what is said in language is that language lacks any
independent being standing over against what is meant in language. The being of language is the speculative presentment
of what is said in it, just as the mirror-reflection is the
appearance of what is there reflected. Insofar as the being of
language is the speculative presentment that occurs in language,
this being fulfills Gadamer's definition of the speculative as
"ungraspable in terms of its own being, and yet throwing back
the picture that is offered to it."[39]

Gadamer's insight into the speculative unity of language
and what is said in language can be deepened by considering the
relation of language and world. By "world" we do not mean any
mere conglomeration of all existing things, nor some structural
totality of all beings. Instead, we mean by this term the
phenomenological notion of the open horizon within which all
beings are manifest. It is the open arena, the openness itself,
which makes possible the standing presence of things.[40]

Given this notion of world, the relation of language and
world can be expressed in the following way. The foundational
openness that first makes possible the coming-forth into appearance of all beings (world) is itself instituted in and as language. To cite Gadamer himself:

> Language is not some item of equipment which is
> made available to man in the world. On the con-
> trary, the fact that man has a world at all is
> itself dependent upon, and present in, language.
> The world as world transpires [*ist Da*] only for
> man, since it occurs [*Dasein hat*] for no other
> living being in the world. But this occurrence
> [*Dasein*] of the world is constituted linguistically.[41]

The claim that the world is itself inherently linguistic in
character is one of the central theses of Gadamer's work.[42] In
this thesis, the ontological import of meaning and language is
clearly affirmed with a radicality that surpasses most if not
all other extant treatments of the nature of language.[43] What
does it mean for Gadamer to claim that the world is itself inherently linguistic? Because of the fact that "world" does not
mean the sum total of manifest beings, this claim does not assert

the absurdity that words are identical to things and things
are identical to words. There is an obvious distinction to be
drawn between words and things.[44] However, the linguistic
constitution of the world *does* mean that *how* things are originally present is first *allowed* in language. In other words,
language is the irreducible *medium*[45] of world-openness, such
that things are present only in words, and on the other hand,
such that words have their being in the things that come-to-
presence in them.

> What comes into language is indeed something other
> than the spoken word itself. But the word is a
> word only through that which comes into language
> in it. In its own sensible being, it is there
> only in order to be taken up completely [*um sich
> aufzuheben*] into what is said. On the other hand
> that which comes into language also is nothing
> that is pre-given nonlinguistically, but rather
> receives in the word its own determination.[46]

Words are the presentments of things, and things come forth as
the meanings of words, both in speculative fashion.

The unity of language and the world can be explicated in
a slightly different way if the question of the "world-in-itself"
is raised. Gadamer rejects as phenomenologically unsound the
notion of the world-in-itself, and in consequence rejects any
notion of world that construes it to lie somehow "behind" language. Instead of this, Gadamer follows phenomenological necessity in identifying the world with the "views" [*Ansichten*] as
which the world occurs.[47] The world is thus, for Gadamer, the
ongoing transmission of the ways that language opens up room
for the appearance of things *as* they are. But these "views" or
world-openings are structured by language, not formally such
that some non-linguistic content is filtered through the forms
of language, but totally, such that everything that is given in
or as the world is first allowed to come forth in the meaning-
relations, i.e., the world-articulations, of language. Thus,
the language that one speaks is one's foundational relatedness
in being, a relatedness that first allows things to manifest
themselves as and how they are. Language is the articulated
openness (world) in which things are present as themselves.[48]

We may now summarize the unity of language and world. The
basic claim advanced here is that language constitutes the

foundational structure or articulation of world-openness. This
means that the meaning-relations which comprise language are
ontologically primary. This, in turn, entails that internally
self-sustained things simply on hand are themselves secondary,
residing in a deeper foundation, since from within their merely
determinate thereness they are unable to supply the basis for
their own meaningful self-showing. What a thing is can be
grasped eidetically only because the essential space for its
manifestation is provided by the speculative opening up of world
which occurs in language. This opening up of world is what
founds the possibility that things may show themselves as and
how they are.

It is time now to summarize those aspects of our interpretation of meaning which can be seen in the speculative unity of
language and what is said in language. In the first place, we
have seen that meaning is always linguistic. And in connection
with this, we have also seen that the linguisticality of meaning
precludes interpreting meaning as either subjective representation or objective content. Meaning is rather the linguistic
occasioning of appearance, and as such it is the unity of language and whatever appears.

Secondly, meaning is essentially constitutive of the world,
rather than a secondary overlay which merely colors or forms
the world. As we have said, the world is the openness of all
appearance, which is itself meaningful. To say that meaning is
constitutive of world-openness is to say that the world is not
open in the way that an empty container or vacuum is open, but
instead that the world is an articulated openness which is
opened up in language in various ways and along various meaning-
channels. These channels of openness are meaning-relations,
specific areas of ontological space. Linguistic meaning occurs
as the holding-open of such areas of ontological space, and thus
as constitutive of world.

Thirdly, the unity of language and what is said in language
reveals a primary characteristic of meaning as such. We shall
term this characteristic "*allowance*." In as much as meaning is
the holding-open of areas of ontological space, meaning is what
fundamentally provides room for the coming into understandable
appearance of whatever is. Meaning *allows* such appearance. To

give but one example of what is meant here, the opening up of
the space of natural objectivity through the linguistic occurring
of nature as a realm of cause and effect is what allows any
given natural object to appear as such. The uncharted and in
many ways yet unseen cosmos that stretches out before our scientific imagination is already allowed to appear as the fabric of
natural cause and effect, only because in language the ontological realm of nature has opened up and is held open. Meaning is
thus primarily characterized as ontological allowance, the
transpiring of the essential space of all appearance.

Meaning as Event: The Speculative Dialectic of the Finite and the Infinite

In addition to the unity of language and what is said in
language, the speculative character of language also entails a
certain dialectic between the finite and the infinite, or to put
it another way, between the definite (finite) possibilities for
self-presentation which language provides and the surpassing of
these possibilities, a surpassing that is always inherent in
the being of language. We are speaking, now, of the "difference"
between language as such and what is said in language, a difference which yet does not nullify or overrule the essential unity
that also obtains between these two. As we shall see, in this
difference between the finitude and the infinity of linguistic
meaning is to be seen the essentially *eventful* character of
meaning. This eventfulness of meaning, moreover, is the institution of primordial time.

Once again, the metaphor of reflection in a mirror may be
used to illuminate this side of the speculative character of
language. We have noted above that the mirror-image shows that
the being of what is reflected is an infinitely open-ended
availability for additional coming-into-appearance. Applied to
language, this metaphor illuminates the *excess* being of language.
By "excess being" is meant that language is always more than
what is said in language, and thus can never be simply identified
with what is definitely said in language (i.e., with the finitude
of language).

If we refer once more to our example of the bookcase, we
may illustrate this side of language's speculative character by

noting the way in which the bookcase presents itself hermeneutically. As we have said, the bookcase is present as something to
be understood in a context of involvements. But is this context
itself something fixed and definite? Is it a closed structure
of involvement? The answer to these questions is no. The context in which the bookcase is meaningful as bookcase is itself
neither fixed nor closed, but instead is open-ended, essentially
incomplete and infinitely expanding. The bookcase gives itself
to be understood as a holder of books, and as such, as a definite
meaning-complex which is the same as the linguistic mediation
of the meaning of bookcase. But the definiteness and finiteness
of this meaning-complex in no way entails any finality with
regard to what "book" means, i.e., with regard to the possibilities of the written word. And this is in addition to the fact
that the bookcase may occur in different contexts as other than
a holder of books, i.e., as shield, as fuel, as aesthetic object,
as sacred shrine. But even in this one aspect, namely the bookcase as presenter of books, the appearance of the bookcase is
speculative, i.e., an appearance which is infinitely open-ended.
The bookcase can never be brought to a full and complete presentation of itself. The context of such presentation is never
closed. Thus there is always "room" for further self-presentation, further hermeneutical or speculative self-giving. Just as
the mirror-image reveals an infinite horizon of ongoing presentation, so the hermeneutical appearance of anything whatsoever
reveals an infinite indetermination in its context of appearance.
Understanding is thus never final and absolute, but ongoing,
speculative. And just as the being of understanding is language,
so language is itself speculative in this sense as well, that
it always means more, intends more, than what is definitely and
finitely said in it.

        It is now appropriate to turn to Gadamer's own discussion
of the dialectic between the finitude (what is definitely said)
and the infinity (the irreducible surpassing of what is definitely
said) of language. We may begin to consider this dialectic from
the side of the finitude of language. Gadamer says the following
in this connection:

        Language is the trace of finitude not because there
        are different types of language structures, but

because each language is constantly being formed
and developed the more it brings its experience
[*Erfahrung*] of the world to language. It is
finite not because it is not all other languages
at once, but simply because it is language.[49]

The central claim here is the one we have just made above,
namely that the coming-to-presence that occurs in and as language is not a consummated state of presentment, but one that
breaks open an indeterminate possibility of further, heightened
presentment.[50]

The background in Gadamer for this claim is his discussion
of the ontological function of the work of art. In this regard,
Gadamer argues that the essence of the picture is presentation
[*Darstellung*], i.e., originary presentment.[51] The work of art
in its pictorialness is misconstrued if seen as a copy, a point
we have already noted with regard to the mirror-image. The
work of art as picture or image does not re-present an original
which remains its guiding criterion of truth. Instead, the
presentation that occurs in the picture is itself "an autonomous
reality" that can only be described as an *increase* in the being
of that which is presented in the picture.

> That the picture has its own reality now means
> that the original [*das Urbild*] comes in the pre-
> sentation to presence. It presents itself therein.
> This is not to say that it [i.e., the original]
> is assigned solely to this presentation in order
> to appear. It can also present itself as what it
> is in other ways. But if it presents itself in
> this way, this is no longer an incidental occur-
> rence but rather belongs to its own being. Such
> a presentation is an ontological occurrence [*ein
> Seinsvorgang*] that helps to comprise the level of
> being of what is presented. In the presentation
> it experiences at the same time an *increase in
> being* [*einen Zuwachs an Sein*]. The intrinsic
> import of the picture is ontologically determined
> as an emanation of the original.[52]

The upshot of this is a more radical conception of presence than
is found in the notion of self-sustained, internal self-identity.[53]
In contrast to this notion, Gadamer's analysis of pictorial presentation suggests that presence may be understood essentially
as self-showing, such that what is present, strictly speaking,
does not belong to itself.[54] In other words, the being of what
is present is not an internal self-containment (substance), but

is rather the "event" of *coming-to*-presence in which what is
present is the same as the speculative presentment itself.
Given this, then the ontological value of the picture can be
understood as an increase in the "pictorialness" of being which
is accordingly an increase in being itself, in the sense of
increased manifestness. "Art as a whole and in a universal sense
brings an increase in 'pictorialness' to being. Word and picture
are not mere imitative illustrations, but allow what they present
to be for the first time what it is."[55]

The preceding exposition of pictorial presentment in the
work of art may be seen to illuminate the finitude of language
in the following way. If the work of art reveals that the
essence of presence is eventful self-showing, then the presentment that occurs in and as language is no longer to be understood
against the ideal of a finally completed or perfected presence.
Instead, linguistic presentment is always coming-to-presence,
the *emergence* of meaning, and as such is always eventful, but
not in the sense of an approach or approximation to an ideal
state of standing presence.

This understanding of linguistic presentment directly entails the finitude of language. Language is finite in that as
the way in which things are given forth, it is not a perfected
completion of givenness but is one originary occurrence in an
inexhaustible process or tradition of such occurrence.[56] One
can now begin to see that this inexhaustibility entails that
the being of language is "more," in a dialectical sense, than
what is said (and thereby revealed) in language. Thus, the
being of language must be distinguished from the concrete presentment that occurs therein, but without any implication that
language thereby becomes something simply other than the presentment itself. In other words, linguistic presentment is not
undialectical, which here means that it is not simply exhausted
in the particular "how" of the presentment, but is rather
speculative presentment.[57]

> To come into language does not mean to receive
> a second existence [*Dasein*]. The way in which
> something presents itself belongs, rather, to its
> own being. Thus, everything that is language
> involves a speculative unity: A differentiation
> in itself, between its being and its self-presenta-
> tion, a differentiation, nevertheless, that is
> also precisely no differentiation at all.[58]

This speculative unity that yet contains a self-differentiation
may also be summarized as follows. What occurs as the understandable presence of something in language is a finite (although
not for that reason imperfect) self-showing of the thing itself.
As we have seen, Gadamer argues that such self-showing does not
occur in the light of an eternal essence that grants to the
thing an essentially non-historical identity, but rather occurs
as a coming-forth that is reflected in the transmission of language itself. And such transmission, which is nothing less than
the history of the being of what is presented in language, is
an open-ended process of tradition (literally "handing on") that
discloses what is determinately presented to be inherently
related to an infinite indeterminacy of further possible presentment. Thus, Gadamer says:

> But there is no possible consciousness--we have
> repeatedly emphasized this, and it is the basis
> of the historicity of understanding--there is no
> possible consciousness, however infinite it might
> be, in which the thing [die "Sache"] that is
> handed down would appear in the light of eternity.
> Every assimilation of tradition is historically
> different--which is not to say that each assimila-
> tion is only an imperfect understanding of the
> thing. Rather, every such assimilation is the
> experience [Erfahrung] of a "view" of the thing
> itself.59

Our presentation of the finitude of language has taken us
to the other side of the dialectic, namely, to the infinity of
language. As has already become clear, "infinity" is not here
conceived as a perfected, eternal state but rather as an indeterminate openness towards the future of the transmission of meaning
in language. In other words, all linguistic presentment has
the character of non-fixity, in that what is presented brings
with it the possibility of further presentment in a different
linguistic context, such that how the thing is itself present
is in a sense changed.

What does this mean? To explicate this, we need to consider again a point that we made earlier to the effect that the
transmission of meaning-relations in language opens up the
"essential space" in which something may come forth as itself.
This "essential space" is, as we have seen, an articulation of
world-openness that provides the ontological "room" for a

determinate self-showing. In making this point, we noted also
that this level of articulated "essential space" is ontologically
more primordial than self-identical presence (determinate givenness). Thus, we moved from the ontic level of internally self-
same *eidos* (the distinctive "whatness" of a thing) to the underlying linguistic allowance of the eventful coming-to-presence
of the thing.

With this as the backdrop, we may now explicate more fully
what the infinity of language entails. When one thinks of a
given thing in the ordinary way, one usually thinks of certain
descriptive features that are themselves characteristic or
distinctive of what the thing is. This is to think of the thing
in terms of its determinate presence. But given that there is a
foundational level underlying determinate givenness, the thing
may be thought of more radically in terms of the features of
this primordium.

We have spoken of the eventful character of linguistic
presentment and have indicated this eventfulness terminologically
in the contrast between presence and coming-to-presence. Now
this contrast needs to be clarified and deepened. The phrase
"the eventfulness of linguistic presentment" does not mean that
a thing in its ontic determinacy occurs as an event rather than
as a presence, if by "event" one means something on the order
of everyday occurrence, such as an automobile accident, a person
walking across a lawn, a tree falling down. There is obviously
an ontic distinction between event in this sense and the self-
sameness of the thing. The thing seems to maintain itself
through the passing away of such occurrences, and thus the thing
must be something different from such occurrences.

What, then, is meant by the eventfulness of linguistic
presentment? To begin with, the notion of "eventfulness" is
here an ontological concept, and thus does not pertain to the
ontic distinction between thing and occurrence. More specifically, "eventfulness" pertains here not to the determinate
givenness of the thing but to the articulated meaning-allowance
that underlies the determinate self-showing of the thing as its
linguistically constituted possibility. This underlying meaning-
allowance itself has the character of non-fixity, in that it
transpires in the transmission of a linguistic tradition. The

crucial claim at this point, however, is that the underlying
meaning-allowance of a thing's self-showing is in truth "conditioned" by the total fabric of meaning-relations that comprise
the linguistic tradition as a whole.[60] Thus, the underlying
meaning-allowance cannot be thought of as an isolable, non-
related possibility, but rather as an intersection in an indefin-
itely extended web of interconnected meaning-relations. This
means that the articulated possibility of a thing's presentment
is dependent upon the total fabric of language. As this total
pattern of relatedness changes, the way in which the thing is
originarily allowed to come forth also changes. Put simply, its
meaning changes, where "meaning" refers to the way something comes
forth in relatedness to everything else.

Another way of saying this is to note that any linguistic
fabric of meaning-relations is pervaded by indeterminacy. Language is thus infinite in that the pattern of world-relatedness
instituted in language has no perfected state, but is rather
open-ended, indefinite, always directed toward the openness of
an indeterminate future. At this point we may recall a passage
that was cited earlier:

> Language itself has a speculative character...as
> the accomplishment of meaning, as the occurrence
> of speech, of communication, of understanding. The
> speculative is such an accomplishment, in that the
> finite possibilities of words are disposed in their
> intended meaning, as in directedness toward the
> infinite. To say what one means, to make oneself
> understood...is to hold what is said together with
> an infinity of what is unsaid in the unity of a
> meaning and to let it be understood as such.[61]

And also: "All human speaking is finite in such a way that
there is within it an infinity of meaning to be unfolded and
interpreted."[62]

This completes our exposition of Gadamer's interpretation
of the essence of meaning. It remains for us in this chapter
to summarize the essential characteristics of meaning based upon
Gadamer's work, and then, finally, to discuss how the inquiry
into the essence of meaning reveals the transcendence of meaning.

Summary: The Essential Characteristics of Meaning

The general claim which Gadamer's work sustains concerning meaning is that meaning is neither subjective nor objective, but is rather ontologically constitutive of world-openness itself, *within* which alone there can be any such things as the subjective or the objective. Within this general claim, we can isolate several essential characteristics of meaning as such.

The first and perhaps most important characteristic of meaning that we wish to indicate is the one that we have already mentioned above, namely, meaning as essential *allowance*. We need not repeat what we have already said in this regard. But we should mention here the essential difference between allowance and cause. As allowance, meaning sustains the ontological space of appearance. But it is not the cause or ground of such appearance. To think allowance on its own terms is not to confuse it with ontic causation, but is rather to understand it as ontological making-room for appearance. Allowance does not ground ontic determination; it does not determine the particularities of whatever shows itself; but instead gives space for this self-showing.

The second characteristic that we wish to call attention to is meaning as *claim*. By characterizing meaning as claim, we wish to state that meaning is not free-floating, but occurs instead in an essential connection with human awareness. Meaning transpires in its eventfulness only as that which lays fundamental claim to human awareness. We discover meaning as that which fashions our awareness in certain basic directions, or to use another metaphor, as that which draws our awareness out into certain general regions of understandable appearance (e.g., nature, ideality, fantasy, the mnemonic). Meaning thus claims human awareness as that which essentially belongs to it. Meaning claims human awareness as its own.

In Gadamer's work, this characteristic of meaning as claim can be gleaned from Gadamer's insistence upon the linguisticality of meaning. Language is obviously an essentially human phenomenon. Accordingly, the essential connection between meaning and human awareness is certainly implied by the doctrine of the linguisticality of meaning. We will have more to say in connection with the claim that meaning imposes upon human awareness, and with the

ownership of human awareness that this claim entails, when we
discuss Heidegger's attempt to think the meaning of being, the
subject of our next chapter.

The third essential characteristic of meaning we wish to
note is meaning as *grant*. By this characteristic is meant the
gift-like character of meaning. Meaning gives itself in human
awareness as the various fields of appearance that human inten-
tional consciousness may occupy, and within which it may become
absorbed. To speak of meaning as grant is thus to deny that
meaning is in any way the creation of human beings or anything
that we fashion for supposedly pre-given purposes or functions.
Instead, we stand in relation to meaning as the recipients of
its self-giving grant to us.

In Gadamer's work, this characteristic of meaning is to be
seen in his discussion of language as tradition, i.e., his
analysis of effective-historical consciousness. For Gadamer,
language is not a human instrument, as we have seen, but is
instead the eventful handing-on of meaning. We are born into
language as tradition, and thus we enter human life precisely in
our inheritance of the gift of meaning in language.

Gadamer uses the notion of effective-historical consciousness to express the human reception of linguistic tradition.
Since we have not explicitly discussed this aspect of Gadamer's
thought, we cite now the following passage:

> The hermeneutical experience is concerned with what
> has been transmitted in tradition. This is what is
> to be experienced. But tradition is not simply a
> process that we learn to know and be in command of
> through experience; it is language, i.e., it
> expresses itself like a "Thou".... [The] effective-
> historical consciousness rises above...naive com-
> paring and assimilating by letting itself experience
> tradition and by keeping itself open to the claim
> to truth encountered in it.[63]

Here we see language described as "Thou," which is to say as
truly independent from one's own intentions, inclinations,
purposes. Here also we see Gadamer asserting linguistic tradition to be a claim to which one must open oneself in order to
experience its truth, rather than anything lying at our disposal.

The final characteristic of meaning that we wish to consider
here is the contrast that obtains between meaning and the

determinate presence of things. Unlike all entities which
come forth in appearance as something particular, meaning does
not come forth to show itself in a determinate presence. Meaning as such is not anything that could come to appearance in   .
this way. Instead, meaning must be characterized as an essential
withholding from determinate presence. Meaning withdraws from
presence, and in such withdrawal sets the stage for that which
does come into self-presentment.

   When we speak of *withdrawal, withholding,* and the like, we
do not mean to suggest that anything that could come to determinate presentment somehow lies behind the scene, hidden and veiled,
yet which could in some infinite state of being come into appearance. On the contrary, we are suggesting that meaning is *in
principle* withheld from presence, even though it institutes the
arena of all possible presence. This aspect of the essence of
meaning draws us close to Heidegger's thought, and accordingly,
we will find in our exposition of Heidegger in the following
chapter an expansion of this discussion of meaning as an essential
withdrawal from presence.

The Transcendence of Meaning

   We shall conclude this chapter on the essence of meaning
with a brief discussion of meaning as transcendent. This work
as a whole is concerned with the meaning of transcendence as
such. Our initial distinction of the *meaning* of transcendence
from the *concept* of transcendent reality led us to inquire into
the essence of meaning. This was necessary in order to determine
the sort of subject-matter that an inquiry into the meaning of
transcendence could possibly have. We have now completed our
interpretation of the essence of meaning. In a later chapter,
we will discuss the special character of transcendence as the
meaning-region of the Holy, that meaning-region in which transcendence gives itself for human concern. However, for the
present we need to consider, on the basis of the findings of
this chapter, how all meaning as such can be characterized as
transcendent.

   In our introduction we said that meaning as such would be
discovered to be transcendent in two senses: first, with
respect to consciousness, and second, with respect to objective

appearance. Now we can see that Gadamer's interpretation of
the essence of meaning indeed sustains both of these claims.
Meaning surpasses in principle all human subjectivity, and hence
human consciousness (including its structural form at any given
time) in that meaning resides in language as tradition, which
human being merely receives. If meaning occurs not as instrument
at the disposal of human beings, but rather as the opening of
an articulated world whose regions call human awareness forth
into their openness, then meaning is primary in relation to human
consciousness. Meaning in principle surpasses the being of
consciousness, and this in an eventful, not a trans-historical
way. This surpassing thus accords well with the primary meaning
of transcendence as surpassing fixed limit, boundary, determination. Whatever the structure of human subjectivity may be
determined to be, meaning is transcendent with respect to it.

On the other hand, meaning is also transcendent with respect
to all objective appearance. Meaning allows the coming forth
of things, not as the ontic cause of such coming-forth, but
rather as the ontological space-provider for understandable
appearance. As world-openness, meaning is thus primary to all
objective presentment, and accordingly is to be thought as
transcendent with respect to such presentment.

CHAPTER III

HEIDEGGER AND ONTOLOGICAL DIFFERENCE

In the previous chapter we have maintained that meaning is
transcendent both with respect to subjectivity and with respect
to objective presentment. But this claim raises the question:
How is it possible to think the transcendence of meaning? On
what basis is thought able to entertain such a claim? Is there
a global fashion of thinking which would encompass both subjectivity and objectivity while according to meaning an equal
primacy with respect to each of these provinces of being?

Our contention in this chapter is that the life-long attempt
of Martin Heidegger to give thought to the meaning of being does
begin to provide just such a global fashion of thinking. Accordingly, our task in this chapter is to elaborate the basic lines
of Heidegger's inquiry into being and its relatedness to human
being, and thus to provide an ontological context for our claim
that the meaning of transcendence is to be sought in the transcendence of meaning.

The task of elaborating the basic intentions of Heidegger's
thought is no easy one. There is no ready access to a so-called
"Heideggerian philosophy" because in a very real sense, there is
no such thing as a Heideggerian philosophy. This may seem a
peculiar assertion to make, particularly since we are avowedly
setting out to elaborate the basic claims of this thinker.
However, it is true to say that there is no such thing as a
Heideggerian philosophy if by this one means that Heidegger
strove throughout his life's work to avoid any "position taking"
vis-à-vis being-as-such. To take a stance in the face of being,
to seek in a scheme of categories (or set of concepts, images,
and the like) to *grasp* the meaning of being, is for Heidegger
to disallow the manner in which being gives itself for thought.
One can indeed squeeze being into categories, models, images,
concepts. And to do this is certainly admissible, in Heidegger's
estimation. He would certainly acknowledge that the subtle
coercion which position-taking imposes upon being is indeed
useful and perhaps enlightening with respect to certain aims.

58   The Meaning of Transcendence

A good example of this is natural scientific research, which
systematically coerces from being as nature certain quantified
answers to pre-formulated questions. In this way, the structure
of natural process is arrived at and secured.

However, Heidegger would remind us that to coerce being
into a revelation of natural structure, or for that matter the
structure of historical process, psychological process, etc.,
is quite different from encountering being-as-such. Being-as-
such is neither nature, nor history, nor the depth of the psyche,
nor pure ideality, nor any other region that is disclosed in
the application to being of some fundamental conceptual adhesion
and the subsequent clarification that results therefrom. Instead,
to encounter being-as-such, one must withdraw in thinking from
the coercion of the concept which yields not revelation of being-
as-such but rather a revelation of some particular field of
presence, some particular yet holistic way that things are given
forth.

How, then, do we engage Heidegger's thought, and how do we
presume to elucidate this thought in one relatively brief chapter? Obviously, we cannot begin to do justice to the many
subtleties and nuances of his many and varied writings. But
perhaps we can hope to unveil the rather simple, underlying
intention of his work as a whole, and to present the few basic
claims that attend this underlying intention.

In order to do justice to Heidegger's own intention, we
must attempt to follow his thought on its own terms. This means
that we must avoid any mere listing of assertions that Heidegger
may have made at one time or another. As we have indicated,
the basic intention of his work cannot be encompassed within a
conceptual assertion or set of such assertions. Therefore, to
divine this intention we must attend not so much to specific
assertions that can be gleaned from his writings, but instead
to the overall direction or "path" which these writings take.
We will try to follow this path not by explicitly tracing the
development in Heidegger's thinking from his early to his later
works,[1] but instead by raising the question of the essence of
understanding, as Heidegger himself did, and seek to find in
this question an entree to the genuine path of Heidegger's
life-long thinking. By so doing, we will hope to move from

the phenomenon of understanding to the thought-realm in which
the meaning of being can first be encountered.

Understanding, Subjectivity and Transcendence

In order to begin our discussion of understanding, we take
note of a fairly obvious fact. Understanding, whatever else
may be said about it, is something that takes place in human
being. Human being and understanding are indissolubly connected.
This fact would seem to indicate that to understand understanding,
one must first understand human being.

How is human being to be understood in its connection with
understanding? In order to focus this question about human
being, we also must take note of another fairly obvious fact:
The field of understanding is the world. By this we mean that
whatever may be understood occurs within the global context of
experience that is usually designated "world."[2] Given this
second fact as well, our discussion of understanding must turn
on the question of the relation of human being and world.

The customary interpretation of human being in its relation
to world has many varied forms, but they all have in common one
basic feature of great importance: They all regard human being
as something discrete, something that is what it is prior to
and independent of its placement within a world of many beings
that are distinct from it. One may regard human being as essentially a physio-chemical organism, or a center of conscious
awareness, or instinctual energy which erupts into conscious
volition, or a spiritual nexus emerging from the vast reservoir
of unconscious, historical experience. But whether one interprets
human being in terms of organism, or consciousness, or spirit,
there lies at the foundation of each of these concepts the
presupposition that hunan being comprises a discrete province
of being, one that may be interpreted independently of analyses
and interpretations of the "world outside." Human being and
the world are presupposed to be external to each other.

The most prevalent concept now in use which reflects this
presupposition of the discreteness of the being of human being
is "subjectivity." When human being is interpreted in terms
of the concept of subjectivity, it is inevitably conceived as
that which stands over against a field of objects. In its

distinction from objectivity, the subject is regarded as essentially self-contained in the sense that it maintains some
structure of internal self-identity that is independent of its
presumably secondary relatedness to the world. Thus, although
the subject may be regarded as having real contact with the
world, or indeed as essentially intending the world as its
inescapable horizon of significance, the subject is nonetheless
still regarded as an internally sustained center of immanence
that is such prior to whatever world-relatedness that it may
also have. What is essential in this view is the assumption
that the subject *is* something that is somehow *internally constituted*, and thus something that can be talked about or described
by itself, in abstraction from its world-involvement.

This interpretation of the subject as in some sense internally constituted prior to its relations to the world has had
serious consequences for the ways in which we seek to understand
and to interpret the world. This can be seen in the so-called
"turn to the subject" that was explicitly dramatized in the
writing of Descartes. This turn brought along with it an
inexorable tendency to appraise everything in terms of criteria
that originated in the presumed immanence of subjectivity.
Chief among these criteria is that of pure and certain knowledge.
If the subject is essentially immanent in itself so as to comprise a center of *direct* and immediate experience that is itself
set over against the full horizon of the world, then such direct
and local experience must become the guiding criterion governing
all human attempts to reach out beyond the local boundaries of
subjectivity in order to discover and to know the world lying
out beyond these boundaries. What this criterion demands is
that the truth, genuineness, reality of anything be shown
through its presentation in direct and immediate subjective
experience, or through valid inferences based upon such experience. Only that which can be validated in this way is to be
accorded the rank of the true, the genuine, or the real.

That this criterion of pure and certain knowledge is tied
to the presupposition of the discrete subject can be readily
seen as follows. The discrete subject is by virtue of its
discreteness comprised of an inwardness of experience. But
this means that experience itself is taken to involve no real

difference, or otherness, for the experiencer and the experienced
are held together in the unity of a singular being. Immediate
subjective experience is thus pure and immediate seeing or "intuition," in which the seeing and what is seen are ontologically
unified. In such pure and immediate seeing, the process of seeing and what is seen are one, such that what is seen is known
purely as such and with absolute certainty.

Furthermore, the discrete subject is contained within its
own limited horizon of immediate experience, which is itself
owned by the subject through pure and certain knowledge. Pure
and certain knowledge is accordingly the subject's self-possession of its own immanent experience. Thus, the presupposition
of the primacy of discrete subjectivity also entails the primacy
of the criterion of pure and certain knowledge, for such knowledge is the mode of the subject's self-identity. The result of
this is that all supposed contact of the subject with that which
is other than it is subordinated to the governing sway of this
criterion. All attempts of the subject to reach out beyond the
boundaries of subjective immanence and identity to discover the
out-lying world must ultimately answer to the demand of the subject that whatever it acknowledge be known on the basis of pure
and immediate experience.

The progressive application of this criterion of pure and
certain knowledge to the various phases of the intercourse
between human being and the world has resulted in the identification of the world as first and foremost a *problem* of knowledge.
The overriding question that then imposes itself in this regard
is: How can the subject know for certain that the world is as
it appears to the subject? How can our immediate "seeing" of
the world guarantee anything beyond the immanence of subjectivity
itself? How can our direct apprehensions be shown to take us
beyond our subjectivity to the very world that is other than us
so that we may know that which lies beyond the immanence which
alone we essentially and immediately inhabit?

There is now, of course, a general recognition that this
epistemological cul-de-sac is telling evidence of the inadequacy
of any notions of subject and world which presuppose a primordial
separation of the two. Thus, numerous thinkers have attempted
to rethink the relation of the subject and the world in a way

that would avoid any essential isolation of one from the other.
But for the most part, these attempts still retain the notion of
subjective immanence or inwardness. Thus, they are forced to
seek a solution to the epistemological problem by construing
immanence or inwardness as somehow continuous with the outside
world. Such attempted solutions must ultimately fail, however,
because the attempt to affirm such continuity runs directly
counter to the conceptual distinction of "inside" and "outside,"
and indeed produces confusion rather than an acceptable solution.
What is needed, therefore, is an interpretation of human being
and world which does not presuppose that human being is essentially "inside" and world essentially "outside" such that the relation of the two is rendered problematic from the outset.

We stated at the beginning of this chapter that the way
in which understanding occurs can be seen to be of considerable
consequence for our interpretation of human being in relation to
world. We have now outlined the customary interpretation of
human being and world, and have seen that it is based primarily
in the notions of subjective immanence, on the one hand, and a
world lying beyond such immanence, on the other. The question
that must now be asked is: How is the occurrence of understanding of consequence for this customary interpretation?

We take the start for our consideration of the phenomenon
of understanding from a generally acknowledged hermeneutical
principle, namely, that any investigation seeking to understand
something must already be directed beforehand toward that which
the investigation seeks to uncover, analyze and interpret. No
investigation can take place in a vacuum. No question can be
raised in complete absence of some already prevailing context
of questioning. In order to question something, to investigate
something, one must already have that something before one in
some available way. One must already have access to the something to be investigated. And this "already having access" is
a way of *already* understanding at the outset that which is to
be investigated. Understanding is already presupposed in any
explicit investigation into anything whatsoever.

With this hermeneutical principle, we have our initial clue
into the essence of the phenomenon of understanding. What does
this clue indicate concerning this phenomenon? To begin with,

it points to the curious character of understanding, a character
which does not fit in well with our standard conceptions and
presuppositions concerning human being and world. To elaborate
this point, we must consider how it is that understanding is
usually thought of, and then contrast this with the curious
character of understanding that is revealed by this principle.
Ordinarily, understanding is construed as *belonging to* the human
subject. In other words, understanding is thought to take place
as a subjective event, something that occurs within the essential
confines of the subject. Understanding is "mental," and thus is
located "in" the human consciousness--as opposed, for instance,
to an event of nature that is presumably "non-mental" or simply
factual.

On the basis of the above mentioned hermeneutical principle,
we have seen that understanding is revealed to be the prior
directedness of an inquiry toward whatever it is that the inquiry
seeks explicitly to investigate. But if understanding is itself
this prior directedness which already encounters in some preconceptual or implicit mode that which the investigation is
seeking to uncover, then understanding is such that it already
lies beyond the subject, reaching out to encompass all possible
"objects" of inquiry. In other words, understanding is here
revealed to be the primordial field *within which* anything whatsoever must already be found that may subsequently become that
towards which one may be directed in explicit investigation.

From this initial indication of the character of understanding, it can be seen that understanding is itself something which
fails to conform to the presumed discreteness of subjectivity as
something standing on "this side" of the actual world. Understanding is certainly something that pertains to human being--
this cannot be denied on any grounds. But the reach of understanding extending beyond the subject to encompass and render
initially accessible all possible objects of investigation--
this reach belies both the identification of human being with
subjective immanence and the identification of world as that
which lies beyond the inward domain of human being. Instead,
understanding seems to extend at once both well within human
consciousness, indeed providing it its foundation, and also
outward throughout the world that is subject to human questioning.

It would thus appear that understanding is confined neither to
the human subject nor to the world in their customary senses,
but is rather a phenomenon that pervades both.

Thus far we have indicated in a preliminary way that the
phenomenon of understanding calls into question our customary
inclination to set human being and world over against each other
by reserving to each a discrete domain that is delimited by the
domain of the other. The next step in our consideration of
the essence of understanding must be to attempt to elucidate
this essence on its own terms, without presupposing any subjec-
tivist bias. Then there must follow an interpretation of human
being in relation to the world that is in accord with the way
in which understanding is itself manifest. However, before
proceeding directly to these tasks, we wish to engage in a
brief excursus concerning the import of the traditional interpretation of human being and world for the question of the meaning
of transcendence as such.

We have noted in our introductory chapter that the root
meaning of the term "transcendence" is "passing beyond fixed
boundary, limit, determination." Now, if the customary interpretation of the relation of human being to the world is adhered
to, then the world must be viewed as transcendent with respect
to human being, since the domain of the world is held to lie
beyond the domain of the human subject. This interpretation of
the meaning of transcendence with respect to the world can be
given more precise formulation if one pays attention to the way
in which the world is thought to lie beyond the human subject.
The world is beyond in that it is *outside*. Thus, its "transcendence" of the subject is a matter of essential *exclusion*. But
what sort of thing is it that lies beyond something else in the
manner of essential exclusion? What is presupposed concerning
the world if the world is held to lie beyond human being by
virtue of its exclusion of the human subject from its full extensive expanse?

The paradigmatic mode in which difference or otherness
occurs in the manner of exclusion is what may be termed *actuality*.
By "actuality" we mean to name *one* way in which beings may be
given, but not the only way. What, then, is the actuality of the
actual? The actual thing is what it is, i.e., attains to

self-subsistent identity, precisely insofar as it excludes what
is other or different from itself. What is other and different
from an actual thing, e.g., some other actual thing, is something
that stands outside the first thing and is thereby excluded from
any involvement in that thing's essential constitution. Thus,
actuality is governed by the principle of *internal* identity.
What an actual thing is is decided solely *within* its own self-
contained region of being, a region that is determined in its
delimitedness precisely by virtue of its exclusion of other
regions, which other regions are thereby likewise determined as
external.

On the basis of this correlation of actuality and the relation of exclusivity, one may anticipate that the interpretation
of the world as essentially excluding the subject presupposes
that the world is something actual or akin to actuality. And
this interpretation is indeed borne out in two ways. First, the
naive talk of an external world (i.e., the world as transcendent
of and essentially excluding the subject) does assume that world
is the total collection of actual things, the places, buildings,
seas, plants, people, mountains, planets, stars, etc., that lie
outside the domain that is immediately owned within subjective
experience. And secondly, the traditional interpretation of
transcendence as attained excellence also bears out the claim
that if transcendence is seen as a relation of exclusivity, the
transcendence will be seen as *actuality*.

Perhaps we may profitably expand this latter point. The
meaning of the term "transcendence" includes, as we have seen,
the sense of qualitative surpassing, i.e., surpassing beyond
accomplished value or merit toward excellence. Traditionally,
this sense of "transcendence" has been seen most fully in the
concept of the perfection of being in God, the absolute attainment of all possible excellences. What we now wish to suggest
is that the actuality (i.e., internal state of attainment) of
the traditional God is implied by the traditional interpretation
of transcendence as exclusivity. If the domain of the subject
essentially excludes the world, then any surpassing of the subject's attained value must in turn lie outside of the ontological purview of the subject. Such surpassing is excluded from
the subject's sphere. But this is to say that transcendence of

subjective value is limited to its own domain by the exclusion
of that which it surpasses. It is limited to the domain of
that which it does not surpass but rather in which it comes to
itself in self-possession. In other words, the exclusion of
transcendence from the realm of subjective attainment forces the
being of transcendence into a domain of self-possessed identity.
But such a domain is a region of actuality in the sense of self-
attained fulfillment. Thus, we conclude that the *actuality* of
the traditional God is entailed by the interpretation of human
being and world as essentially exclusive of each other.

If what we have said to this point is valid, then it would
seem that any basic reinterpretation of the relation of human
being to world will also bring in its train a reinterpretation
of the meaning of transcendence. We have just seen that transcendence in the sense of the actual transcendent (self-fulfilled
perfection of being) has its roots in the interpretation of the
relation of human being to the world as a relation of essential
exclusion. But such an interpretation is tied up with the claim
that human being is essentially located in the immanence of
subjectivity, an immanence which sustains its self-identity in
exclusive independence of its secondary world-relatedness. Thus,
an interpretation of human being which is not based in the notion
of subjective immanence and a corresponding reinterpretation of
the relation of human being to the world should result in an
understanding of transcendence which is quite different from
the traditional notion of a transcendent actuality. Indeed, we
hope to advance just such a reinterpretation of the meaning of
transcendence, one which has significant implications for one's
understanding of transcendence as a religious and theological
theme.

Heidegger and Understanding

Our overall task is to understand the meaning of transcendence as such. But what we have discovered to this point is
that our clue to unlocking this meaning is provided by the phenomenon of the understanding. This clue comes to light in the
following way. The essential character of transcendence rests
in the way in which otherness or difference occurs. With regard
to human being, what is ostensibly other and different is the

world. Thus, any interpretation of transcendence is linked to
the *way* in which human being is seen to be related to the world.
It is at this point that understanding itself enters the picture,
for understanding occurs in such a way as to call into question
our customary ways of interpreting the relation of human being
and world. Accordingly, an elucidation of the essential character of understanding will provide the context within which
the meaning of transcendence may be understood.

It is now time to turn our attention directly to Heidegger.
What we wish to do first is to introduce Heidegger's own discussion of understanding as it occurs in *Sein und Zeit*, and then
turn to a discussion of two fundamental discoveries which
Heidegger made concerning the essential character of understanding.

The narrow focus of Heidegger's discussion of understanding
takes place in section 32 of *Sein und Zeit*. Here, the possibility of an explicit or thematic interpretation of something is
seen to reside not in the mere application of concepts or categories to pre-given brute material, but rather in the fact that
what is to be interpreted is always already understood in some
primordial, pre-reflective way. Moreover, such primordial,
pre-reflective understanding is itself constitutive of how one
finds oneself situated in the world, i.e., how one is fundamentally with things in a comprehensive, relational context.[3]

The central claim that Heidegger advances here is twofold.
First, he claims that understanding (*Verstehen*) is different
from and more primordial than any pure seeing or pure perception
(*Anschauung, Wahrnehmung*) that simply beholds the on-hand givenness of some objectivity.[4] And secondly, he claims that the
essential character of understanding is the preconceptual awareness of something in its temporal network of world-extensive
relatedness, a network that inherently includes the thing's
involvement in its own matrix of possibility.[5] Thus, understanding in this sense is not a subject's mere appropriation of, or
perspective upon, some given objectivity that is substantially
independent both of its presence to the subject and of its
inherent involvement in possibility. This is to say that the
meaning of a thing is found in a primordial pattern of relatedness which itself comprises the articulated openness of the

world, including the openness of the future as it occurs in
the anticipatory thrust of the thing's possibility.[6] And understanding is itself our inheritance of this pattern of relatedness, an inheritance which itself preserves the open continuity
of the whole of world-openness. Understanding thus underlies
the derived distinction of subject and object, in that it is
the world-extensive interinvolvement or connectedness among
things. In short, Heidegger's claim is that consciousness or
mind is literally inherited as the fundamental, relational
totality of the world.

In addition to this explicitly focused discussion of the
phenomenon of understanding, Heidegger also provides in *Sein
und Zeit* two further discoveries concerning the essential character of understanding. One of these discoveries concerns the
radical "level" at which understanding takes place, and the
other concerns the "place" or "locus" that understanding essentially occupies.

First, we shall consider the level at which understanding
takes place. It is commonplace to assume that understanding
occurs at the level of intellectual comprehension. If this were
the case, then to understand something would mean to grasp it
via the intellect. Such grasping occurs through the mediation
of the concept. The concept, in turn, is a universal possibility
that is somehow given for the use of the intellect. To understand something is thus to apply such a universal possibility
to some individual occurrence or situation, so as to see this
universal possibility exemplified therein. Thus, the conflation
of understanding with intellectual comprehension entails that
understanding is the wedding of the concept with the individual
or particular instance.

If understanding is taken to occur at the level of conceptual intellection, then understanding is interpreted as consciousness which overlays the given contents of the world with some
sort of conceptual significance. Over against this view,
Heidegger has suggested that understanding occurs at a much more
radical level, a level that precedes and indeed first makes
possible any such thing as conceptual intellection. We have
already seen the reason for Heidegger's denial that the level
of understanding is the level of conceptual intellection: the

understanding that first opens up access to a possible direction
of inquiry is itself the prior basis for conceptual or thematic
investigation.

The level at which understanding itself occurs is termed
"Dasein" by Heidegger.[7] Whatever else this term is intended to
mean, it is clear that Heidegger uses the term to name the
essential happening, i.e., the being, of human being.[8] Therefore, if Dasein is the level at which understanding occurs,
understanding is itself at least partially constitutive of the
being of human being, such that whenever and wherever human being
occurs, there understanding occurs. And if this is true, there
is thus no such thing as human being which is not understanding;
the two are the same.

But to say that the level at which understanding occurs is
Dasein, the very being of human being, is not yet to say what
the "place" of understanding is in the sense of its essential
range or extent. As to the place of understanding, Heidegger
proffers an equally radical claim. The commonplace view of the
locus of understanding is the conscious mind. Understanding is
taken to be something mental, and accordingly the mind is taken
to be the place wherein understanding is located. This means
that the extent to which the mind reaches determines the parameters of the locus of understanding.

Before considering Heidegger's alternative to this commonplace view, we wish to expand on its implications. Mind is
usually assumed to mean the rationally ordered conscious awareness of the human subject. Wherever the conscious subject is
rationally aware, there one finds mind. But the human subject
is taken to be individualized and particularly located by virtue
of the centering of consciousness in a definite spatio-temporal
embodiment. Hence, the mind of the individual subject is also
taken to be particularly located. To be sure, it is allowed
that consciousness extends far beyond the actual material
reaches of the body, and so mind is not held to be confined,
even in the commonplace view, to the body's physical dimensions.
But nevertheless, the consciousness of mind is taken to be
rooted in the sentient apparatus of the body, and in consequence
of this mind is itself held to emanate from a center that is
defined by an individual body's location, insofar as it is

carried along on the back of consciousness. Thus, mind invades
the world, casting its light upon it, and yet its constitutive
light remains rooted in a particular subjective center of
consciousness.

The crucial point in this interpretation of mind as the
locus of understanding is that mind is seen to be a particular-
ized source of lumination that illuminates certain accessible
structures of the world in a fashion analogous to a searchlight
of a certain color which shines out into the darkness and illuminates objects whose color reflects the particular color of
the searchlight. What this analogy reveals is the assumption
that mind is something that is in addition to the world, something that happens in addition to the hidden and dumb "thereness" of the world's contents. Mind enters a pre-given world
of nature, of brute force, and through its luminescence lights
up the structure and content of that world. But mind is secondary to world, and essentially independent from it.

We may advance this exposition of the commonplace view of
mind and understanding one step further. Because the multiplicity
of individual and specifically located minds is itself limited,
the world as a seemingly unlimited and inexhaustible field of
brute "thereness" is taken to be extramental. It could be on
this view that any given part of world is in fact illumined by
the light of mind. But such need not be the case. Indeed,
unless one posits an infinite mind, one must presume on this
view that there are vast reaches of world (e.g., the far reaches
of intergalactic space, or the infinitesimal reaches of the sub-
atomic) that have never been illumined or are just now undergoing
illumination by mind. Thus, understanding is taken to penetrate
the world in a somewhat haphazard fashion, and always after the
fact of the world's apparently unlimited brute thereness.

The basis of Heidegger's rejection of this commonplace view
is the insight into the impossibility of separating mind as
awareness from the supposedly pre-given "thereness" of world.
To say that the world is "there" is utterly unintelligible except
as an indication of the situation of awareness. No matter how
one is focally aware, whether in the mode of perception, or
memory, or imagination, the location of such a mode must already
have emerged in awareness. In other words, for something to

be "there" means that it is already given in the being of awareness and is thus already available for some mode of focal atten-
tiveness.

The question now arises as to how one ought to interpret
the availability of anything in its thereness for some mode of
focal attention. For Heidegger, this availability must be
interpreted in terms of the disclosedness of human being. Human
being in its disclosedness must already encompass the field of
possible thereness in order for any focal attention to take
place. But the field of possible thereness is none other than
the entirety of the world itself. Thus, human being in its
disclosedness must encompass the world, i.e., must be world-
extensive. This foundational, unified encompassing of world by
human being Heidegger has named "Being-in-the-world" (*In-der-
Welt-sein*).

We may now relate this to the question of the essential
locus of understanding. We have already seen that Heidegger
does not use the term "understanding" to name conceptual intellection, but rather something that occurs at the ground level of
human being, which he terms "Dasein." In what sense, then, is
Dasein the occurrence of understanding? To say that Dasein is
the occurrence of understanding is to say that Dasein is the
primordial disclosedness of possibility.[9] What this means is
that understanding is the foundational occurrence of possibility
as the received structure of our world-awareness. But what is
the context of the possible? Such a context must be broader
than the totality of the actual, for in Heidegger's thinking
the possible outstrips the actual.[10] This context must be
broader than the actual and yet also inclusive of it, for whatever is actual is also obviously possible. The term which can
legitimately name this context is "world," because its global
extension can include all possible bearing upon human awareness.
The locus of understanding, then, is for Heidegger not individu-
ally located consciousness but the very world itself, in its
extension beyond actuality into possible-being.[11]

Understanding, for Heidegger, is thus the preconceptual
extension of human being throughout the world-extensive field of
possibility. In understanding, therefore, is revealed the fact
that human being is not subjectively confined, but is world-

extensive, already occupying the primordial sphere of possible-being.

At this point, we may relate our current discussion of Heidegger to our previous discussion of meaning as treated by Gadamer. In our consideration of the essence of meaning, we have maintained that meaning as such can be characterized as transcendent. This has suggested to us that the essence (i.e., *how* it transpires as such) of transcendence is to be discovered in the essence of meaning. For purposes of relating this to our current discussion, we may say that meaning occurs as possibility in Heidegger's existential sense of being-possible. However, we have seen that being-possible occurs as Dasein, which we have already established to be the being of human being.

What all this would seem to suggest is that transcendence must accordingly be interpreted in terms of the being of human being. Does this not mean that transcendence must be interpreted within an anthropological context, and does this not therefore involve a "humanization" of transcendence? As we shall see, this interpretation of Heidegger's analysis of Dasein must be rejected, as the following will show.

We have already noted that for Heidegger, understanding is constitutive of the being of human being, and that the essential locus of understanding is the world itself. These two claims must now be deepened in order to approach what Heidegger intends the term "Dasein" to name. To say that understanding is constitutive of human being is to say that human being is co-extensive with understanding. And this is to say that human being is world-extensive.[12] But the world is understood as the region of all possible coming-forth and coming-to-stand, in short, the region of anything that can possibly be. Hence, the world-extension of understanding means that Dasein as understanding is already and always an understanding of being as such.[13]

But what does this mean? Again, understanding does not here mean an "interpretive" grasping of that which is given beforehand. Instead, it means the primordial occurrence of what is to be interpreted, occurrence that bears toward us and in this bearing-toward first grants the possibility of our comprehending it. Thus, understanding as such must be the total field of all such bearing-toward, a field that must be named being.

Understanding is the occurrence of being itself in its bearing-toward, and is not any subjective coloring or illumination of that which is pregiven. But understanding is also a fundamental way that human being happens. Accordingly, the relation of human being to being itself is seen to be an intimate one, one that cannot be grasped in terms of our ordinary conceptions of relation. The question that must now be addressed is: How is one to understand the relation, comprised in part by understanding, of human being and being as such?

The "Relation" of Human Being to Being-as-such

If understanding is both an essential feature of the fundamental way that human being is, on the one hand, and yet also the way that Being itself occurs in its "bearing toward" on the other, then the essence of understanding reveals that human being cannot be understood at all apart from its essential relatedness to being-as-such. In fact, one must say that human being is essentially nothing other than relatedness-to-being, with such relatedness comprising the very heart of human Dasein.[14] But more than this needs to be said. Just as one cannot understand human being except as relatedness-to-being, so also one cannot understand being-as-such except as relatedness to the essence of human being.[15] Neither the essence of human being nor being-as-such can be understood except in their relatedness to the other. This relatedness is itself primary; human being "by itself" or being "in and for itself" are both abstraction from the primal occurrence of this relatedness.[16]

The term "Da-sein" names for Heidegger this very relatedness as opposed to human being taken by itself or being-as-such taken in and for itself.[17] As Heidegger himself has said:

> In order to indicate in a single word both the
> relation [Bezug] of being to the essence of man as
> well as the essential relation [Wesensverhältnis]
> of man to the openness or "here" ["Da"] of being
> [Sein] as such, the name "Dasein" was chosen for
> the essential domain in which man stands as man.[18]

Thus it can be seen that to identify Da-sein as the unsurpassable context within which the meaning of transcendence as such is to be sought is not a reduction of this meaning to anthropology, nor is it a "humanization" of this meaning. This much follows

from the fact that Da-sein is not at the disposal of man, nor
limited in any way to some sort of subjective sphere or merely
human standpoint. It is for this reason that Heidegger says at
one point: "the essential occurring [*das Wesen* (verbal)] of
man, 'the Dasein in man,'...is nothing human."[19]

Da-sein is the foundational relatedness in which there first
occurs human being and anything else that is in being. But can
this relatedness itself be further characterized? Because
Da-sein is the relatedness in which human being and being-as-
such belong to each other, Da-sein is not anything that can be
described in terms of ordinary appearance or definite self-presentation. Da-sein does not itself occur as a circumscribed
specificity, because this latter type of occurrence is always
set over against and delimited by other occurrences of the same
sort. But Da-sein is precisely all-embracing in relation to
particular, circumscribed occurrence. To characterize Da-sein
therefore, one must avoid all description that pertains to what
is bounded and thus delimited in its particularity by that which
occurs additionally outside and beyond it.

The characterization that Heidegger initially gave of
Da-sein and which lays the basis for his later, continued use
of the term can be briefly summarized in the following manner.
Da-sein is not anything that comes forth in definite (i.e.,
bounded) self-presentment after the fashion of particular beings
that are within the world, but is rather the "site" where all
such beings are present, or come into their originary manifestation. Da-sein is thus the prevailing of the manifestness of
what is manifest, the "happening" of an encompassing place which
first gives room for the coming-forth of whatever presents itself as itself. Da-sein, therefore, *is* disclosedness, the unconcealment which happens as truth.[20]

But how does such a "place" happen, a place that is itself
not bounded by any other places because it is the basic site of
all possible locations? We have already seen that the happening
of this foundational site is something that pertains at once and
essentially both to human being and to being-as-such. To be
sure, Da-sein cannot be collapsed into either of these "parties,"
for it is itself the relation or dimension that underlies their
distinctiveness. Accordingly, it would be ideal to proceed at

once to a characterization of Da-sein as such, without even
considering its distillation into the contrast of human being
and being as such. However, our long-engrained habits of thought
do not allow us to escape so easily from our habit of understanding all things in terms of their ontic particularities. Therefore, we will approach a characterization of Da-sein from each
of its two sides, with the hope of showing how each side already
includes the other and thus leads into Da-sein as such. The two
sides have been referred to by us as "human being" and "being-
as-such." But our starting point will in each case be provided
by a key notion or term which conveys the essence of the respective side. In the case of human being, this key notion is
existence. In the case of being-as-such, the key notion is
coming-to-presence. By pursuing the meaning of these two sides
through these two notions, the way will be cleared for a more
adequate characterization of Da-sein itself.

We will begin with the side of being-as-such. In Heidegger's
estimation, the term "being" [*Sein*] is neither the emptiest of
all concepts, nor is it a term whose meaning is obvious and
discernable from any direction. To entertain the meaning of
being is rather for Heidegger extremely difficult, and indeed
not fully a matter of human effort. But nevertheless, being-as-
such has shown itself throughout the history of Western thought
in terms of a fundamental character. "Since the earliest times
of the Greeks up to the latest times of our century, being has
meant: coming-to-presence [*Anwesen*]."[21] The first thing to
note here is that *Anwesen* in German is a verbal noun, and thus
its meaning is to be distinguished from what is present, from
the condition or state of standing presence. Being is different
from this in that it is coming-to-presence, emergence into
presence. How are we to understand this difference? At one
point Heidegger says the following:

> Seen in terms of beings, the standing-forth
> [*Vorstellen*] of beings is already and always
> something that surpasses beings. For instance,
> if we stand facing a cathedral [*stellen wir z.B.
> das Münster vor*], what stands forth for us is not
> merely a church, a building, but rather something
> that is present precisely in its coming-to-presence
> [*sondern Anwesendes, nämlich in seinem Anwesen*].
> The coming-to-presence of what is present is thus
> not something that in the end we *also* stand facing,

> but is rather what *precedes*. It stands before us
> prior to all else, but we do not see it because we
> stand within it. It is what genuinely comes forth
> for us.[22]

In this passage, Heidegger claims that being, i.e., coming-to-
presence, precedes what is particularly present, and thus is
primordial with respect to the specific presentment of some
particular thing, such as the church building. It is the "prior
foundation" of specific presentment.

The question now arises as to how such a "prior foundation"
is to be understood. The prevalent way that such "foundation"
has been interpreted in our metaphysical tradition is permanent
presence, the state of already-being-present. And this, in turn,
has been understood as the eternal being which is prior to all
temporal emergence.[23] However, for Heidegger such an interpretation of being involves a fateful "forgottenness" of being as
coming-to-presence in its difference from the beings which show
themselves as they stand in their presence.[24]

How, then, may we understand coming-to-presence as that
which is primary to all specific presentment? To begin with,
coming-to-presence is certainly never separable from what it is
that comes forth as present. There can be no coming-to-presence
except insofar as something thereby attains a definite presentment: "If we say 'being,' then this means: 'being of beings.'"[25]

But coming-to-presence is both different from and primary
with respect to specific or particular presentment. It is not
simply *what* is determinately present, but is rather the allowance of what is present, the letting-come-to-presence of what
is present.[26] How does this letting-come-to-presence itself
occur? It occurs as the primordial trait which lets beings
emerge into their specific manifestation. It is the primordial
"setting-free" of things into the openness of co-present beings.
With regard to this primordial letting-come-to-presence, Heidegger
writes:

> Taking the original sense of the word as our point
> of departure, letting [*lassen*] means: to let go,
> let go away, put away, let depart, that is, to set
> free *into the open*. What is present, which has
> been freed by letting-come-to-presence, is only
> thus admitted as something present for itself into
> the openness of co-present beings.[27]

It should be noted that this primordial trait of letting-come-to-presence is neither a metaphysical cause nor a transcendental condition, but is rather a pervasive feature of what is present itself. It is the allowance as such of all definite emergence into unconcealment, the freeing of that which is set free into presence, the pervasive character of all that is which lets what-is manifest itself in an open domain of manifestation. It is the unconcealment itself which allows what is unconcealed to show itself in its definiteness.[28]

Thus far, the allowance, the letting, which characterizes coming-to-presence has been discussed in relation to the beings that are allowed into their definite presentments. But there is an additional way in which letting-come-to-presence is to be understood. Not only does the primordial allowance pertain to the free emergence of beings in their particularity, their determinate emergence into the openness of co-present beings. In addition, primordial allowance pertains as well to the very transpiring of coming-to-presence, to the very realm of manifestness in which things are manifest. But this means that primordial allowance is a letting, an allowing of being itself over and above the allowing which sets beings free in their particular presentment.[29]

At this juncture, we have come upon an initial indication of the inadequacy of discussing being-as-such as if it were something on its own. We have seen that being-as-such is nothing but the allowance that lets beings emerge into the open manifestation of their particularity within the openness of co-present beings. But this allowance, i.e., the emerging manifestness of what is manifest, is itself allowed for. It itself prevails as the being of beings. But if one seeks to give thought to this prevailing, one is in a sense taken beyond the characterization of being as letting-come-to-presence. Being-as-such thus leads thought beyond its own prevailing character.

In order to secure this point, we must anticipate something of our later discussion in this chapter. Being, letting-come-to-presence, cannot be understood on its own, for a thoughtful consideration of the meaning of being as coming-to-presence leads, in Heidegger's estimation, to the foundational *granting* which gives the prevailing character of being as coming-to-

presence, and which accordingly cannot itself be understood in
terms of coming-to-presence. Heidegger uses the following
German term to name this foundational granting of the character
of being: *Lichtung*. Later one, we will have occasion to discuss this term in detail. For the present, we need only note
the primacy accorded to *Lichtung* in relation to being as coming-
to-presence in Heidegger's thinking:

> The clearing [*Lichtung*] grants before all else the
> possibility of the path to presence [*Anwesenheit*],
> and grants the possible coming-to-presence of that
> presence itself.... The peaceful heart of the
> clearing is the place of stillness from which
> alone the possibility of the belonging together
> of being and thinking, that is, presence and
> perceiving, can arise at all.30

Thus we see that being-as-such passes over into a dimension that
cannot be comprised within the meaning of being as coming-to-
presence. And yet it is this dimension which itself comprises
the full meaning of Da-sein.

We began this discussion of being-as-such with the anticipation that it would intrinsically pass over to the other "side"
of foundational relatedness, i.e., the side of human being. This
passing over has not yet been explicitly revealed, and yet the
initial indication, given above, that being-as-such inherently
passes beyond to a more basic allowance of coming-to-presence
itself has prepared the way for the intrinsic move to human
being. How this is can now be shown.

The inherent relatedness of being-as-such to human being
can be understood from a further reflection upon the meaning of
being as coming-to-presence. Coming-to-presence is itself the
allowance of determinate manifestation. But the meaning of such
allowance must include a *reception* of such emergence. Indeed,
there could be no such emergence without some reception of what
thereby emerges. And this is to say that being itself is essentially empty without a corresponding recipience of that which
is allowed in letting-come-to-presence. The allowance of
determinate manifestation is thus inherently involved in the
reception and preservation of this allowance. Where does such
reception and preservation take place? It takes place on the
side of human being. Accordingly, we find in Heidegger that
discussion of being as coming-to-presence always involves a

discussion of man as the one who essentially receives the gift
of such coming-to-presence.

> Man: standing within the approach of presence,
> but in such a way that he receives as a gift the
> coming-to-presence that is given [das es gibt] by
> perceiving what appears in letting-come-to-presence.
> If man were not the constant recipient of the gift
> given by "the giving of coming-to-presence," if
> that which is extended in the gift did not reach
> man, then not only would being remain concealed
> in the absence of the gift, not only closed off,
> but man would remain excluded from the scope of
> the giving of coming-to-presence. Man would not
> be man.[31]

Without the essential receipt of the allowance that yields what
is determinately manifest, being-as-such would evaporate into
complete darkness and absence. Being-as-such thus devolves into
its relation to human being.

We may now turn to this side of primordial relatedness, the
side of human being as such. The primary terms which Heidegger
uses to characterize human being as such is "*existence*." As we
shall see, the meaning of existence also inherently involves the
meaning of being-as-such. But at the outset, at any rate, the
term "existence" is used to emphasize the fact that the foundational site of all possible occurrence (i.e., Da-sein) itself
transpires as the essence of man. Accordingly, we will begin
with this emphasis and follow its own inherent devolution into
primordial relatedness itself.

In *Sein und Zeit*, Heidegger states that "the 'essence'
[*Wesen*] of Dasein lies in its existence [*Existenz*]."[32] This
statement is then discussed in his "Brief über den 'Humanismus',"
written some twenty years later. In this later work, Heidegger
says of the statement quoted from *Sein und Zeit*:

> But ek-sistence [*Ek-sistenz*] thought in this way
> is not identical to the traditional concept of
> *existentia*, which signifies actuality in distinction
> from *essentia* in the sense of possibility....On
> the contrary, the statement [of *Sein und Zeit*] says:
> man essentially prevails [*west*] such that he is the
> "here" [*Da*]...of being. This "being" of the "here"
> and only this has the fundamental character of
> ek-sistence, which is to say: ecstatic standing
> within the truth of being.[33]

Because the statement in *Sein und Zeit* lent itself to misinter-
pretation, Heidegger in his later writings changed the spelling

of the German term from *Existenz* to *Ek-sistenz* thereby emphasiz-
ing its root meaning. That root meaning is "standing-out," and
thus it names the *ecstatic* character of human being, the ecstatic
dwelling of human being that is out beyond any and all body
locations, out beyond the determinate location of any particular
actuality.

One way of elucidating what Heidegger means by the ecstatic
character of human being is to consider what he has to say concerning space. In one lengthy section in an essay entitled
"Bauen Wohnen Denken," he explicates the relation of man and
space.[34] His first point here is that it is incorrect to think
of space either as something that is outside of man, or as an
inner experience of man. "When we speak of man and space, it
sounds as though man stood on one side, space on the other. Yet
space is not something that stands over against man. It is
neither an external object nor an inner experience."[35] But if
space is neither external to man, nor an inner experience, how
is the relation of space to human being to be understood? His
answer to this question is suggested in the following passage:

> If all of us now think, from where we are right
> here, of the old bridge in Heidelberg, this thinking
> to that location is not a mere experience inside
> the persons present here; rather, it belongs to
> the essence of our thinking *of* [*an*] that Bridge
> that *in itself* [*in sich*] thinking *persists through-
> out* the distance to that location. From here,
> we are out there at the bridge, and by no means
> are we at some representational content in our
> consciousness.[36]

In this phenomenon of thinking out toward and at something that
is physically far away, the ecstatic character of human being
is disclosed. Heidegger's claim here is that to encounter in
thought (memory, anticipation, imagination, etc.) something that
is not directly perceived because of its great distance from
one's body and its sense organs is nevertheless *to be out with*
that something, even though one does not perceive it directly.
This *being out with* obviously does not mean that one is out there
alongside the thing in any physical or ontic sense. But it does
mean that in a non-physical, ontological sense, human being is
out along with the things encountered in thought. In other words,
this *being out with* reveals that human *being* already pervades the

locations at which anything can be present. Human being already
persists throughout the space in which things are present (or
absent, for that matter, in the perceptual sense). Accordingly,
human being is already pervasive of primal space. Thus Heidegger
says:

> Spaces and with them space as such are always granted
> [*eingeräumt*] already within the abode of mortals....
> And only because mortals pervade, in their very being,
> spaces are they able to go through spaces.... I am
> never here only, as this encapsulated body; rather,
> I am there, that is, I already pervade space, and
> only thus can I go through it.[37]

This *being out with* as it applies to space is also in
Heidegger's estimation the primary feature of human being as
such. Man ek-sists, not because he is existent in the ontic
sense of determinate actuality, but because he stands out beyond
the containment of all immanence.

As ek-sistent, man stands out beyond his bodily location,
beyond the possible locations of all particular beings, and
inhabits the primal abode of all coming-to-presence.[38] And
indeed, it is precisely this habitation which holds open this
abode, and thus allows coming-to-presence (being) to prevail.
"Man holds open the place...so that in its Openness there can
be given coming-to-presence (being)."[39] Thus, the allowance of
coming-to-presence takes place as the essential human occupation
of the abode of such coming-to-presence, an occupation which
first sets this abode free into its openness.

Just as human ek-sistence is an inherent aspect of being-
as-such, so also human being does not occur independently of
its ecstatic standing-out into the open abode of being. The
occupation by human being of the abode of coming-to-presence is
not something that happens "after the fact" of the being of
human being. Rather, such occupation is itself the founding
occurrence of human being that first grants to man whatever may
be deemed his "essence." Man is essentially constituted only in
and as the ecstatic occupation of the open abode of being.

What this means is that man as such cannot be essentially
determined apart from his founding surrender to the prevailing
of being as coming-to-presence. Human being itself is thus *not*
a discrete region of being, but is essentially handed over to the

preservation of the meaning of being. Any independent "essence"
of man is thus swallowed up in the essential human task of holding open the abode of being.

As the prevailing of the presence of what is present, being
is literally what *overpowers* the being of man. This overpowering is suggested by Heidegger in the following:

> The Da-sein of historical man means: to be set out
> as the breach in which the overpowering emergence
> of being bursts into its appearing, so that this
> breach itself shatters against being....Dasein
> is the breach through which there transpires the
> opening up of being which is thereby set into
> play in beings [*des ins Werk gesetzen Seins im*
> *Seienden*]. As such, Dasein is an episodic falling-
> between [*Zwischen-fall*] in which suddenly the
> unbounded and overwhelming power of being emerges
> and comes into play as history.[40]

What is noteworthy about this passage is the claim that Da-sein,
here meaning essential human being, *shatters* against the overpowering emergence of being. This means that human being is
literally *nothing* in itself--it is totally delivered over to the
presencing of that which is given forth in coming-to-presence.
Human being as such is merely a breach, a "falling-between,"
which is wholly comprised in the emergence of being. Thus,
human being as such, thought in terms of ek-sistence, devolves
into the preponderant grant of being-as-such.

This understanding of human being completely undercuts any
characterization of human *being* as essentially subjectivity.
Man is not a subject that stands on this side of world, but is
rather already "thrown" out into "the openness of being, which
openness first illumines the 'between' within which a 'relation'
of subject and object can 'be'."[41] To be a subject means to
intuit, to perceive objects. But in Heidegger's thinking, the
basic "perceiving" of beings is not anything belonging to the
subject.

> Beings are not in being because man first intuits
> or regards them in the sense of representation
> in the mode of subjective perception. Much rather
> is man the one who is regarded [*Angeschaute*] by
> beings, the one who is gathered into beings by
> their self-opening unto their coming-to-presence.[42]

Man perceives beings only because the self-opening of beings has
already occurred in Da-sein, such that beings emerge facing man,

presencing themselves to man, and gathering him into their
presence. And such gathering occurs as the ecstatic devolution
of ek-sistence into the preserve of being; thus it is prior to
any conceivable subjectivity.

To this point we have maintained that man "occupies" the
open abode of coming-to-presence and in this devolving occupation first finds his ek-sistent "essence." But something more
needs to be said concerning this occupation. The ecstatic
standing-out which is named "ek-sistence" is a standing out
beyond all possible beings into the disclosedness that first
lets beings show themselves as and how they are, that first lets
beings be. Ek-sistence is thus the preserving of the essential
allowance of beings themselves in their determinate manifestness.
But such preserving is precisely freedom, the primordial absence
of imposition or constraint. Hence, the letting-be of beings
which occurs in the preserving of human ek-sistence is the primal
institution of freedom, which itself is the allowance of the
disclosedness of whatever is as and how it shows forth.[43]

In order to elucidate further this notion of letting-be in
relation to ek-sistence, we may turn to a correlative notion,
that of *Entschlossenheit*.[44] Heidegger uses this term, not in
its ordinary German sense of volitional resolve, but rather in
its root meaning: "unlocked, being open to."[45] *Ent-schlossenheit*
thus names for Heidegger a concrete possibility that each human
has, namely, the possibility of standing open to one's foundational Da-sein, the possibility of being attuned to one's
ecstatic ek-sistence. Such a concrete state of accord between
one's concrete "self" and one's primordial Da-sein is not at all
guaranteed, or even possible as a fixed and enduring state.
This is because for the most part, human being is absorbed within and captured by the determinate particularities which beings
manifest, and the culturally sanctioned concerns which pertain
to such particularities.[46] But in contrast to this, there is
also the elusive possibility of breaking free of this absorption
and thereby becoming immediately aware of one's primary dwelling
in the abode of Openness itself. "*Entschlossenheit* is not the
deliberate action of a subject, but rather the opening up of
Dasein, out of its absorption in beings, into the Openness of
being."[47]

Because *Entschlossenheit* is the concrete occurrence of
human being in immediate awareness of its own founding Da-sein,
the state of *Entschlossenheit* is the revelation of human being
as and how it essentially is. *Entschlossenheit* is the "transparency" of human being in which human being is disclosed to ek-sist
into the freedom which lets beings be.[48] But the elusiveness of
Entschlossenheit indicates that concrete human being rarely
attains in awareness to his own foundational occurrence. In
spite of such elusiveness, however, it is nevertheless the rare
attainment of *Entschlossenheit* which provides descriptive warrant
for the claims regarding the character of Da-sein.

As ek-sistent, man stands *out beyond* the determinate particularities of beings *into* the freedom which lets beings be,
and which thereby allows them to manifest themselves in their
originary self-showing. Thus we see that ek-sistence is both a
"standing-out-beyond" and a "standing-into." It is a standing-
out-beyond relative to the particularities of determinate beings
and it is a standing-into relative to the openness, the allowance of being itself.[49] The importance of adding the notion of
"standing-into" or "standing-within" [*Inständigkeit*] to the
ecstatic standing-out of ek-sistence is clearly stated by
Heidegger as follows:

> The ecstatic essence of existence is still not
> adequately understood if one represents it only
> as "standing out" [*Hinausstehen*] such that the
> "out" [*hinaus*] is taken as the way out of the
> interiority of an immanence of consciousness and
> spirit. Understood in this way, existence would
> still be represented in terms of "subjectivity"
> and "substance," while the "out" remains to be
> thought as the openness of being itself which has
> the character of being-outside [*als das Auseinander
> der Offenheit des Seins*]. The stasis of the
> ecstatic consists--as strange as it may sound--
> in the standing-within in the "out" and "here"
> [*Da*] of unconcealment as which being itself
> essentially prevails [*west*]. What is to be
> thought in the name "existence"...can be designated
> most beautifully with the word "*Inständigkeit*."[50]

From this one can readily see that man's ek-sistent occupation
of the world, of the open abode of being, is not simply a
standing-out-beyond, but is also a standing-within the ecstatic
reaches of coming-to-presence itself. Thus, *Inständigkeit* names
the devolution of human being to the meaning of being-as-such,

and is accordingly that aspect of ek-sistence that points most directly, from the "side" of human being, to the primacy of foundational relatedness itself.

What remains to be discussed concerning man's relation to being is the basic character of the relation itself, given that the relation is itself primary even with regard to being-as-such and human being as such. But what can be said directly of this primordial relation that does not fall into the respective emphases of either one or the other of the two sides?

One of Heidegger's more extended discussions of the relation itself that prevails between man and being is found in his essay "Der Satz der Identität."[51] The basis for the thinking that takes place in this essay is provided by a famous fragment of Parmenides, which in Greek reads: *to gar auto noein estin te kai einai.* Heidegger's reading of this fragment differs from the customary one, according to which an identity of being and thinking is here affirmed. Instead of this customary reading, Heidegger interprets this fragment to say that thinking and being both alike belong to the Same.[52] The question that this fragment thus provokes for Heidegger is the following: How are we to think the "sameness" to which both being and thinking (i.e., human being) belong?

The clue to thinking this sameness is provided for Heidegger by the meaning of *belonging.* Ordinarily, one thinks of belonging as belonging together. Likewise, one thinks of belonging together in terms of the *togetherness* of what belongs together. But "togetherness" names a kind of co-ordination or association of two or more things, a bringing into relation of that which is otherwise apart or separate. Hence, belonging is ordinarily thought of in terms of the association of what is otherwise independent of such association.

However, this way of thinking about belonging is inadequate for the belonging which prevails between thinking (human being) and being itself (coming-to-presence). It is inadequate because it accords primacy to *what* belongs together rather than to the belongingness itself.[53] But if one thinks not in terms of *what* it is that belongs together, and instead attempts to think of *belonging* as itself primary, then such thinking begins to move in the direction of the "sameness" to which both thinking and being belong.

How, then, does one think of belongingness itself, the belonging in terms of which alone both human being and being-as-such can be adequately understood? We will return to Heidegger's discussion of the primacy of belonging as this discussion is found in the essay "Der Satz der Identität." But in the meantime, it may be helpful to turn to several other of his essays in which this primordial relatedness enveloping both human being and being-as-such is discussed.

At numerous points in his writings, Heidegger has attempted to characterize this primordial belonging without allowing the emphasis to fall either upon the side of being-as-such or the side of human being. One of these attempts revolves around a particularly pregnant word with a variety of meaning-overtones. This word is the German *Not*, a word which conveys among others the following senses: "need," "want," "necessity," "peril," "distress," "urgency." One is thus tempted to translate this term with a compound phrase, such as the following: "the urgent and perilous necessity of need." However, such a lengthy phrase used to translate a single word would result in rather awkward English renditions. We will therefore avoid such a construction when we translate Heidegger's use of this term into English, but it should be kept in mind that all of these senses are intended when this term occurs in Heidegger's work.

In order to see how this term is used to characterize the primordial essence of belonging, two rather lengthy passages need to be reproduced here:

> Man, however, is pressed [*genötigt*]into such Da-sein, is cast into the necessitating need [*Not*] of such being, because the overpowering as such, in order to hold sway in its appearing, requires for itself the abode of Openness. The essence of human being is first opened up for us only when it is understood in terms of this "need" which is necessitated [*ernotigt*] by being itself....
> Because they [the Greeks], in the unique need [*Not*] of their Dasein, used only violence and so did not eliminate the need but rather increased it, they won for themselves the fundamental conditions of true historical greatness....
> Being [here, *physis*], the overpowering appearing, necessitates through its need [*ernotigt*] the gathering which takes hold of and grounds human being.... 54

> Instead of calculating beings in terms of beings,
> it [essential thinking] expends itself in being for
> the truth of being. This thinking answers to the
> "claimful address" [*Anspruch*] of being, in that
> man surrenders his historical essence to the simpli-
> city of the unique, urgent necessity [*Notwendigkeit*]
> which does not coerce through forceful constraint
> but rather produces the necessity of need [*Not*]
> which is fulfilled in the freedom of sacrifice. The
> necessity of need is that the truth of being be
> preserved, whatever may befall man and all other
> beings. The sacrifice, which is raised above all
> forceful constraint because it arises from the abyss
> of freedom, is the expenditure of human being in
> the preserving of the truth of being on behalf of
> beings.55

What one notices in each of these passages is that both man as
such and being-as-such are themselves understood in terms of
the "urgent necessity of primordial need," a need that precedes
them both. Being-as-such is, as we have seen, the emergent
(here: "overpowering") eruption into presence of *what* is present
(i.e., beings). This emergent eruption the Greeks named *physis*.[56]
But emergent eruption into presence is not anything in itself or
by itself, as we have also seen. Instead, it is preceded (not
temporally, but rather *essentially*) by the necessity of need.

In the first of the passages cited above, Heidegger seems
to suggest that the need does fall on the side of being-as-such.
However, we may regard this as Heidegger's attempt to avoid an
existentialist humanization of the meaning of being. In the
second passage, however, it is clearer that Heidegger understands
the necessity of need to be the primordium with respect to being-
as-such. Being-as-such, coming-to-presence, is preceded by the
urgent, necessitating need for a "site" for such coming-to-presence or emergent eruption into presence. The need itself cannot
be understood within the scope of emergent eruption into presence,
because it is the need for a "site" within which such coming-to-
presence will prevail. As need for such a site, it is essentially
primary to being-as-such.

On the other side of the coin there is human being, which,
as we have seen, is essentially understood as ek-sistence. But
human being as well cannot be understood on its own for it also
is preceded by the need which invokes, necessitates the open
site that man in his ek-sistent being essentially preserves
through an equally essential "sacrifice" of any tendency toward

reduction to merely ontic self-preservation.[57] The needful
requirement of such sacrifice indeed places human being "in
peril," for under the sway of this need man cannot determine or
possess his own being. Instead, man is "in peril" because he is
thrown beyond himself into the awesome task of preserving the
open place of being that is invoked by such primal need.

At this point we can state more fully why it is that the
need does not simply reside on the side of being-as-such. The
need that we are speaking of is the need for ek-sistence, a
need that necessitates the ecstatic character of ek-sistence.
But this "necessitating" is not the sort of compulsion that could
be said to lie on the side of being as some sort of principle or
transcendental requirement. The term "*Not*" does not here name
a necessity in the sense of a fixed structural requirement of
being, but rather the needful necessity *that is such only* in the
fulfillment of man's essential sacrifice. It is a necessity
which is in need of man in order for its very necessity to prevail, in order for there to be any necessity or urgency at all.
Thus it is only the sacrifice, the belonging of human being to
the need, that allows the need to prevail at all. But this
means that the need engulfs the two sides of being and human
being, or to put it better, underlies the distinction of the
two sides as the primordial sameness of belonging. Accordingly,
it may be said that the term "*Not*" names the relatedness, the
primordial dimension in whose belonging-in-sameness there first
occurs ek-sistent human being, on the one hand, and emergent
eruption into presence (*physis*, being), on the other. Each of
these "sides" belongs to the sameness of the need, a sameness
which itself, in turn, transpires only in the belongingness of
the two sides.

Another word used by Heidegger to characterize foundational
relatedness is "gathering."[58] At one point, Heidegger says the
following: "Being itself is the relation, insofar as it gathers
to itself and sustains ek-sistence in its existential, that is,
ecstatic essence as the site of the truth of being in the midst
of beings."[59] At first glance, this sentence seems to ground
the relation of being and human being in being-as-such. But
actually the sentence says something different from this. It
says that the relation itself gathers or collects ecstatic human

ek-sistence into the task of providing room for the truth of
being. In this context, the truth of being names coming-to-
presence, i.e., the *disclosedness* of whatever is present. Thus,
the gathering is a collecting of human being into the sustained
requirement of preserving such disclosedness. The gathering is
thus in a sense primary both with respect to ek-sistence and
with respect to coming-to-presence.

In support of this conclusion, another passage may be cited
which indicates that "gathering" names the relatedness that is
primordial: "It is possible that what touches us and approaches
us, insofar as we attain to our human being, does not need to
be represented, constantly and specifically, by us. Nevertheless
...it is gathered beforehand *toward* us. In a certain sense,
we are this gathering itself, although not exclusively."[60] Just
as the earlier passage did not ground gathering in being-as-such,
so this passage does not ground gathering in human being. Neither
being-as-such nor human being is the one which does the gathering.
Rather, the term "gathering" names the primary "coming together"
or collectedness into ecstatic unity, in terms of which there
can first be any such thing as human being or coming-to-presence.

Another of Heidegger's characterizations of primordial relatedness centers in a term that is quite prominent in his writings, namely, *Lichtung*. Heidegger uses this term to designate
the primordial allowance both of being-as-such and human being.
At an earlier point in this chapter we noted that allowance is a
trait of being as coming-to-presence in that coming-to-presence
is itself the allowance of the determinant manifestation of
beings in their particularity. However, allowance is more than
this character trait of being-as-such. In addition to this,
there is also the more fundamental allowance of being itself
(in distinction from beings in their particularity). Coming-to-
presence is the "overwhelming" emergence into open manifestation.
As such, it is the pervasive presencing of beings in contrast
to their particular standing presence. Such pervasive presencing, however, is an issuing-forth and this means an issuing-
forth from the hidden "source." This "source" is not to be
construed metaphysically as first cause or as anything lying
"behind" emergent presencing, but is rather to be described in
its claimful involvement with human awareness. This hidden

"source" is itself the *allowance* of coming-to-presence in its
inherent involvement in human Da-sein, an allowance which
Heidegger terms *Lichtung*.

We may begin our discussion of the meaning of this term by
considering its etymological overtones.[61] The term bears the
primary meaning of "clearing," as in a clearing in a dense
forest. It thus means an opening within density. The verb
lichten, from which *Lichtung* is derived, means "to lighten" in
the sense of "to unburden," "to make easy," as in "to lighten
one's load." Thus, *Lichtung* names the foundational *enabling*
that occurs as a lightening, as an unburdening into freedom and
openness.[62] The basic sense of "clearing" means that foundational enabling is the clearing of openness in density, which
thus provides a free space whose transparency rises up out of
impenetrable opacity, a free space which is itself cleared of
determinate specificity. Particular beings are present in
their determinacy as limits to free transparency. They are not
themselves enabling because as particular things they are not
lightening openness but rather in their sheer givenness are
ultimately inscrutable, opaque, impenetrable, non-enabling.
But in addition to the sheer givenness of things, there is also
the free opening that enables by clearing room. This is *Lichtung*,
an unburdening of sheer density, sheer mass, through the grant
of primal freedom.

The German adjective *licht*, in addition to meaning "light"
as the opposite of "mass" or "density" or "heaviness" also means
"light" in the sense of brightness, as in "a light room." The
term *Lichtung*, however, is not etymologically related to this
second sense of *licht*. Thus, *Lichtung* does not mean luminosity
itself. Luminosity is indeed a character to be accorded to
being-as-such, for coming-to-presence is the allowance of determinate manifestation. But *Lichtung* is intended to name the prior
grant of the luminosity or unconcealedness of beings. "Light
can stream into the *Lichtung*, into its openness, and in this
openness brightness is allowed to play with the darkness. But
light never first creates the *Lichtung*. Rather, light presupposes
the *Lichtung*."[63] *Lichtung* is thus what enables being-as-such,
i.e., luminous coming-to-presence, to transpire.[64]

In a particularly expressive passage, Heidegger gives the
following account of the meaning of *Lichtung*:

> Beings stand in being i.e., in their unconcealed-
> ness ....And yet, beyond beings, not away from them
> but prior to them, something else takes place. In
> the midst of beings in their totality there tran-
> spires an open place. There is an enabling clearing
> [*Eine Lichtung ist*]. Thought of in terms of beings
> [*Seienden*], it is more in being [*Seienden*] than
> beings. This open midst is therefore not enclosed
> by what is, but instead the enabling, cleared midst
> itself encircles...all beings.[65]

Lichtung is pervasive; it "encircles" the coming to and abiding
in presence of all particular beings. But because of this, it
does not itself come-to-presence as do beings, although it is
more basic to what-is than beings themselves are. Thus, Heidegger
says that "the *Lichtung*, in which beings stand, is in itself at
the same time concealment."[66] As the allowance of coming-to-
presence, *Lichtung* is not itself such as to come forth in unconcealment, but remains hiddenness, mystery. A little further on
we will have more to say concerning concealment. For now, we
wish merely to note that as concealment, *Lichtung* is primary
even with regard to being-as-such (unconcealedness).

We may conclude this discussion of *Lichtung* with one further
passage:

> *Lichtung* grants before all else the possibility of
> the path to presence and grants the possible coming-
> to-presence itself.... The peaceful heart of the
> *Lichtung* is the place of stillness from which alone
> the possibility of the belonging together of being
> and thinking, that is, presence and perceiving, can
> arise at all.[67]

This passage summarizes what we have been saying with regard to
primordial relatedness as *Lichtung*, namely, that such *Lichtung*
is the enabling *grant* of the belonging together of being-as-
such (coming-to-presence) and human being (here: thinking).[68]
The *Lichtung* is primordial with regard both to being-as-such and
human being.

We need to note at this point that this discussion of
Lichtung brings us full circle back to our earlier discussion of
Da-sein. We stated earlier that the term "Da-sein" names the
relatedness of human being and being-as-such, where this relatedness is itself primary with respect to the two "sides" (see

above, pp. 73-75). Now we see that *Lichtung* is the way that
Da-sein occurs, i.e., as enabling clearing, and that in addition,
it can be characterized as both "necessitating need" and as
allowance. Having discussed these ways of characterizing primordial relatedness (Da-sein), we may now return to Heidegger's
discussion of primordial belonging as this occurs in his essay
"Der Satz der Identität."

The point at which we wish to renew our discussion of this
essay is a pregnant passage in which Heidegger sums up much
that we have said above concerning the relatedness of man and
being:

> The distinctive character of man is that as the
> being who thinks, he is open to being, is set
> before being, remains drawn to being and thus
> answers to it.... A belonging to being prevails
> within man, a belonging [*Gehören*] which listens
> to being [*auf das Sein hört*], because it is
> appropriate to being. And being? If we think
> being according to its original meaning as
> coming-to-presence, being presences for man
> neither incidentally nor occasionally. Being
> presences and abides only insofar as it has to
> do with man through its claim upon him. For it
> is man, open to being, that allows the arrival
> of being as coming-to-presence. Such coming-to-
> presence requires the openness of an enabling
> clearing [*Lichtung*], and by this requirement
> remains appropriated to human beings.[69]

In this passage, Heidegger clearly indicates that both human
being and being-as-such are appropriated to each other, belong
to each other, and hence cannot be understood except in terms of
their relatedness to each other. In what we have said to this
point, we have given some characterization to this primordial
relatedness, but in every case, such characterization has
amounted to a *via negativa*. We have characterized this relatedness as *necessitating need*, but such characterization is in
terms of the need for ecstatic human ek-sistence. We have
characterized this relatedness as *allowance*, but this characterization is in terms of the room provided for the coming-to-
presence and abiding disclosedness of particular beings. And we
have characterized this relatedness as *enabling clearing*, but
this characterization is in terms of the openness whose indeterminacy grants the possibility of determinate coming-to-presence.
In each of these cases, the characterization of primordial

relatedness (Da-sein) is in terms of that which is other, i.e., is in terms of its *difference* from beings and their determinate disclosedness. But is there a way of thinking which avoids this *via negativa*? Is there an immediate and direct encounter with Da-sein that avoids the manner of thinking which must mediate Da-sein through the thinking of the difference?

Immediately following the summary passage which we have just quoted, Heidegger states that we stubbornly misunderstand the *belonging* together of man and being as long as we try to think this belonging through categories or mediations of any kind. But even our own rendering of Heidegger's words in the above exposition may very well classify as a mediation through the difference of Da-sein from beings and their disclosedness. But what other way of thinking is there, if even our use of Heidegger's own words fails to pass the test that he himself sets up?

Heidegger's answer in the essay we are now considering, "Der Satz der Identität," is a peculiar one, at least from the point of view of thinking which seeks to *represent* some truth. For in this essay Heidegger urges that to think the *belonging* of man and being, our thinking must leap away both from man and from being and enter what from within the horizon of meta-physical, representational thinking can only be termed as *Abyss*.[70] But the encounter that takes place in such a leap or spring is the encounter with that belongingness in which we already find ourselves, and so it is not an abyss into which we leap if by "abyss" is meant a void that lies beyond our being.

How, then, does this encounter with belongingness take place? How does one "leap" into a direct encounter with primor-dial belonging?

The Encounter with Da-sein as No-thing

In Heidegger's early writings, an answer is supplied to the above question. In these writings, Heidegger suggests that a specific mode of human awareness can occur inwhich one is directly aware of Da-sein. As we shall eventually see, this awareness is of a preliminary sort, one which leads to the en-counter with Da-sein but does not, as it were, encounter in full Da-sein's own self-characterization. Da-sein is here revealed,

but not yet fully on its own terms, or as we would prefer to
say, not yet in its fully divine character. In any event, we
must consider this way of encountering Da-sein before considering
how else Da-sein also gives itself to be experienced.

Heidegger's discussion of this preliminary mode of awareness of pure Da-sein is most readily found in his essay "Was
ist Metaphysik?" In this essay, Heidegger begins with the
necessity of differentiating the kind of awareness which encounters Da-sein from the awareness that encounters beings.
Science (*Wissenschaft*) in the broad sense names the various
modes of thoughtful involvement in and analysis of the things
that are. Thus, "Was ist Metaphysik?" seeks to uncover a mode
of awareness that is inherently non-scientific, one that is
aware beyond the particularities of what-is. But if science is
the sum total of our knowledge of whatever is, what other sort
of awareness might there be?

Heidegger answers this question by pointing to a mode of
awareness that is ordinarily termed "mood." But as is so often
the case, Heidegger highlights etymological overtones that are
dormant in the German term so that its usual or everyday sense
is transformed by the interlacing of these overtones. The German
term here, whose ordinary sense is equivalent to the English
"mood," is *Stimmung*. However, it is etymologically related to
the German *Stimme*, which among other things means "voice." It
is also related to the cognate verb *stimmen*, which means both
"to tune," and "to be in accord with," "to be in tune with."
The term *Stimmung* thus does not mean "feeling" in the sense of
interior or merely subjective sensation, but rather names the
affective state of being attuned to something, being in tune
with the "voice" in which something declares itself.

These etymological relationships support Heidegger's claim
that at least some of the states that are ordinarily named
"mood" in the sense of feeling, or mere interior sensation, are
really states of fundamental accord obtaining between human
being and that which is giving itself voice in the primary "tone"
of such attunement. In other words, *Stimmung* for Heidegger names
a type of awareness that is not dependent upon the intellectual
grasping of something (i.e., cognition), but is rather the awareness that takes place through an attunement in which one's being

moodfully resonates within the harmonic register of a primary
sounding, a voice that "vibrates" in one's mood.

That which voices itself in such attunement is not the
human subject, for such moodful attunement occurs not as something "inside" but rather as awareness which is all-encompassing
of both "inside" and "outside."[71] Thus, Heidegger's claim is
that it is descriptively accurate to characterize at least some
moods as world-encompassing states, states which reveal in a
non-scientific or non-cognitive manner, the non-thingly wholeness that surrounds and envelops the particulars in our experience.

It is just such a moodful attunement that provides an entry
into the preliminary awareness of that realm from which the
mutual belonging of being and human being stems. This moodful
attunement Heidegger names "*Angst*." But before one identifies
Angst with what is ordinarily termed "anxiety" or "dread," one
needs to pay attention to Heidegger's descriptive account of
the awareness that this term is intended to name.

The context in which Heidegger introduces the term "*Angst*"
is, as we said previously, the question of an awareness that
goes "beyond" our experience of particular things. The totality
of particular beings exhausts what is. Thus, we are speaking
of an awareness that goes beyond the *totality* of what is, which
goes beyond the singular matrix of disclosedness in which things
are meaningfully manifest, i.e., manifest within a world-extensive pattern of purposive interinvolvements. When Heidegger
speaks of the *totality* of what is, he means this singular matrix
of disclosedness, which we can also identify as being, coming-
to-presence. The awareness that Heidegger terms "*Angst*" is an
awareness that stretches beyond disclosedness as such, that is
not limited to the presencing, the manifestness, of what is
manifest.

The awareness that goes beyond the disclosedness of all
that is is an awareness which dwells in the realm of the primordial "other" to the totality of what is. Such awareness dwells
in the realm that is other than the disclosedness of all that
is, and hence that is "other" than being-as-such, insofar as
this names the manner of disclosedness, the coming-to-presence,
of what is. In short, *Angst* dwells in the realm that negates

disclosedness, that negates the *totality* of what is. But how
can one speak of a realm that negates the totality of what is?
Only one term can name such a realm, and that term is "Nothing,"
"*das Nichts*." Thus, Heidegger's discussion of *Angst* is governed
by his attention to the full reach of this moodful attunement as
it reaches out into--Nothing.[72]

It is now time to consider Heidegger's description of *Angst*
which by reaching out into Nothing reveals the realm that is
other than the totality of particular beings. To begin with,
Angst occurs as indefinite, non-directed, pervasive. It is not
correlated with any particular contents or areas of experience.
How then, can it be described? *Angst* takes place as a non-
localized sense of being cast out of the familiar, a sense of
universal uncanniness, a loss of the comfort of being at home
in one's experience. So at least initially, *Angst* comes over
one as a radical sense of displacement, of being displaced not
with regard to any thing or setting in particular, but of being
displaced *with regard to one's experience itself*. One is no
longer intimate with the contents of one's experience, whatever
they might be, but instead feels estranged, distanced, from the
total context of disclosure, and not merely from something
particular that happens to be disclosed.

This sense of uncanniness and estrangement vis-à-vis
disclosedness itself Heidegger terms "*Unheimlichkeit*" (being-
not-at-home). "In *Angst*, we say, there is not-at-homeness['*ist
es einem unheimlich*']."[73] But this sense of being-not-at-home
is indeterminate, and not in the sense of a merely incidental
lack of determination, but rather in the sense of that which is
in principle beyond determination, that which is essentially
indeterminate.[74] Thus, the being-not-at-homeness of *Angst* is
a disclosure not of anything determinate but of the indeterminate
as such. It is a global shift from the disclosedness of the
determinate to the engulfing suspense of Nothing, the No-thingly,
the Other. As Heidegger says:

> In *Angst*,...all things and we ourselves sink into
> an indifference. But not in the sense of a mere
> disappearance. Instead, in their receding things
> turn toward us. This receding of beings in their
> totality, which presses around us in anxiety,
> oppresses us. There remains no hold. In the
> slipping away of beings, there remains and

comes over us only this "no hold." *Angst* reveals
the Nothing.75

Here we see *Angst* described as the slipping away of beings, in
whose slipping away is revealed that what prevails offers no
hold, no solid anchorage. Instead, there is only pure suspense,
the uncanniness of the indeterminate.

When Heidegger speaks here of "the Nothing," he does not
mean any mere void or absence of beings. In *Angst*, therefore,
the experience of beings is not erased. Beings themselves are
not annihilated. Instead, they become indifferent, unable to
claim one's moodful attunement, unable to draw one into involvement with the presencing of beings, and thus into the purposiveness of the world of their appearance. The totality of beings,
and this means the world-wide tissue of their interinvolvements,
becomes superfluous, tenuous.

> In *Angst* beings-in-their-totality become tenuous
> [*hinfällig*]. In what sense does this happen?
> Beings are certainly not annihilated through
> *Angst* so that nothing remains.... Rather, the
> Nothing announces itself with and in beings
> expressly as a slipping away of the totality.76

The Nothing is an indeterminate suspense that transpires moodfully in the very midst of beings. And this indeterminate suspense reveals the total structure of purposive interrelations
in which alone beings of whatever sort may provide "hold" for
man, to be free-floating within this primordial suspense.

Furthermore, the revelation of this suspense can be described as a radical sea-change in which the customary relational
structure of world itself becomes the strange, "unmeaning" in
the sense of "failing to claim human awareness for itself."
At one point Heidegger says:

> The Nothing itself does not draw toward itself,
> but instead is essentially refusing. But this
> refusing of itself as such is, however, a referring
> to the sinking totality of beings *which lets it
> slip away.* This wholly refusing which refers to
> the slipping away of the totality of beings, as
> which the Nothing in *Angst* presses around Dasein,
> is the essence of the Nothing: nihilation....
> Nihilation is not a fortuitous occurrence.
> Instead, as the self-refusing which refers to
> the totality of beings that is slipping away, it
> reveals these beings in their full but previously
> concealed strangeness as what is radically Other--
> with respect to the Nothing.77

This passage says: The Nothing as nihilation is "other" than
coming-to-presence, other than the being-as-such of what is
present. And it is "other" than human-being-as-such in that it
is the refusal of the essential human task of preserving the
way in which disclosedness (i.e., truth, as in the Greek "*a-
letheia*") prevails. And yet, in *Angst* human being itself ek-
sists out within this Nothing, ecstatically beyond the pale of
coming-to-presence as such, and beyond the pale of the human
task of preserving the manner of such presencing.

    Angst is thus a direct awareness of primordial hiddenness
or concealment. *Angst* brings one into the dimension of *mystery*
out of which both being-as-such and human being emerge in their
belongingness. Da-sein, primordial relatedness itself, must
accordingly be thought *as* this hiddenness, this mystery. Da-sein
is "more" than coming-to-presence in that it is withdrawal-from-
presence. Da-sein is mystery not in the sense of that which
might eventually or in principle be unhidden or drawn out of
mystery, but instead in the sense of that which is inherently
and essentially irreducible mystery. Mystery lies at the very
heart of the disclosedness of beings and its preservation in
ecstatic ek-sistence. And insofar as disclosedness is truth
itself, the *essence* of truth, the "deepest heart" of truth, is
hiddenness, which is to say, *non-truth*.

> Da-sein, insofar as it ek-sists, preserves the first
> and widest non-disclosedness, authentic non-truth.
> The authentic non-presencing [*Un-wesen*] of truth
> is the mystery.... Even in insistent ek-sistence,
> the mystery holds sway, but as the forgotten and
> thus non-presencing [*unwesentlich*] essence [*Wesen*]
> of truth.78

The direct encounter of Da-sein in *Angst* is the encounter with
mystery, with the non-truth lying at the very heart of truth,
and with the ultimate "limits" of being-as-such as preserved
in human ek-sistence. It is thus the primordial encounter with
the "finitude" of the belongingness of being and human being to
each other.

Meaning and Transcendence

We may begin to draw some conclusions from our consideration to this point of Heidegger's thinking pursuit of the experience and the understanding of Da-sein. Our hope is that this
pursuit provides good indication of the global context within
which transcendence itself can be understood.

The conclusion to Chapter II was that meaning is transcendent in character both with respect to objective presentment
and with respect to consciousness. Now we can see how this
transcendence of meaning is to be thought in terms of Da-sein.
Meaning is grant, allowance, claim. Meaning grants the openness
of world by claiming human ek-sistence as the preserve in which
is allowed the disclosedness of beings. However, meaning as such
surpasses its character of grant, allowance, claim. It does not
grant itself any open place of presentment. It does not allow
itself to come to presence. It does not claim human being for
its own disclosure as something or other. Indeed, if meaning
were to "accomplish" any of this it would no longer be named
"meaning." For meaning is essentially the "other" to all that
comes-to-presence in the open preserve of human being. Meaning
surpasses being (coming-to-presence, disclosedness) in its character of withholding-in-mystery. Meaning transcends being by
failing to have any determinate center, by failing to attain to
any self-consistent stand. Meaning transcends being by failing
to be exhausted in disclosedness, any matrix of disclosure, or
truth. Meaning thus transcends truth. Meaning transcends in
that it is the ultimate no-thingly undisclosedness, *the non-
truth in which all open disclosure is irreducibly suspended.*

Transcendence is this non-truth, this nondisclosedness
which lies even "deeper" than being and truth themselves. It
is the Nothing which is primeval and which alone allows the openness of all that is, the openness of being itself. Transcendence
is the transcendence of meaning in that meaning essentially surpasses its own character by extending into the primeval "dark"
of Nothing.

An obvious implication of this, one that we have mentioned
before, is that transcendence cannot be thought within the
restricted ontology of the actual. There is no "reality" to
transcendence if "reality" means that which attains to internal

self-identity (whether simply *or* dialectically) and thus can
come to a stand which entails coming-to-presence. Transcendence
is accordingly not such as to become fixed in any structure of
disclosedness. There can therefore be no transcendental investigation of transcendence. Transcendence is rather the radically
non-fixed, the lack of self-identical stance, that which is
other than the actual--the real (although not, for that matter,
of less importance than the real).

Another way of saying this is to state that transcendence
reveals no stoppage of language in determinacy. The essential
character of language as infinity-within-finite-presentment
remains unsurpassable. The transcendence of meaning is the
transcendence of the saying of language, the indeterminable
hidden "source" of the emergence of meaning in language. It is
the radically inexplicable character of the "destiny" of meaning
which resides in language.

Thus far, we have seen that Heidegger's thinking pursuit of
Da-sein shows that transcendence, if thought on its own terms,
is not the accomplishment or fulfillment characteristic of the
actual, but is instead the primordial Nothing that pervades the
actual as the mysterious suspense within which all actuality is
given forth. However, we have also stated that the experience
of Da-sein (transcendence) as Nothing and as primordial mystery
is itself preliminary. Indeed, to experience transcendence as
irreducible mystery is to experience Da-sein, but it is not to
encounter the special "self-giving" of Da-sein as divine, a
"self-giving" which does not in any way undercut the hidden
mystery of Da-sein but which alters the basic way in which human
being experiences its own relation to this hidden mystery. As
the experience of this relation alters, Da-sein is experienced
differently, not simply as mystery but also as divine. Thus,
we can speak of the *special* way in which Da-sein is to be encountered. This special way is the self-giving of Da-sein in
the claim of the Holy, one of the primordial "meaning-domains"
as which Da-sein may transpire.

In the next chapter, we will consider Heidegger's later
account of Da-sein as articulated into several primordial and
interplaying domains of meaning. As we shall see, .the Holy is
one of these domains, and indeed is the one in which transcendence

64874

gives itself *in its divinity* through an alteration of the
experience that humans may have of the primordial realm of
Da-sein. This will then pave the way for a characterization
of divine transcendence that goes beyond the language of mystery
and hiddenness without, however, undercutting such language.

CHAPTER IV

THE HOLY AS THE MEANING-ALLOWANCE
OF TRANSCENDENCE AS SUCH

In the previous chapter, we have advanced several phenomenological claims which are central to our attempt to inquire into the meaning of transcendence as such. In order to smooth the way into the subject-matter of the present chapter, we offer a summary of these claims in the following list.

1. Transcendence, in the sense of "surpassing fixed limit, boundary, determination," is a characteristic of meaning as such.

2. Meaning as such transcends the particular appearance of what is present in that it is the *allowance* of what is present.

3. Meaning as such transcends human consciousness (subjective immanence) in that meaning *grants* itself to human being as gift to be received through the "total mediation" of language.

4. Meaning as such is nevertheless not independent of human being (not a separate reality) in that meaning transpires as that which lays *claim* to human ek-sistence, thereby drafting it into the need to preserve the open domain in and as which alone meaning may prevail.

5. The open domain of meaning's prevailing, held open by the preserving ek-sistence of human dwelling, is itself *world*, the place of all possible appearance.

6. The ultimate "character" of the place of all possible appearance cannot finally be understood simply in terms of being itself (coming-to-presence), or simply in terms of human being (ecstatic ek-sistence), but must be understood instead as the *primordial relatedness* of the two (i.e., as Da-sein).

7. This primordial relatedness cannot ultimately be described in any satisfactory way because Da-sein is essentially *withdrawal from presence*. In *Angst*, the primordial domain of meaning is revealed to be the inherent and irreducible mystery that pervades determinate, particular presence.

Transcendence and Irreducible Mystery

This last claim, the irreducible mystery of Da-sein, provides the starting point for the present chapter. If Da-sein,
the primordial domain of meaning, is ultimately irreducible
mystery, then the transcendence of meaning is also mystery
itself. In a sense, then, transcendence as such must be thought
as the transcendence, the literal surpassing, of meaning. Meaning as such is allowance, grant, claim. In each of these characterizations, the transcendence of meaning (subjective genitive)
is revealed. But if the primordial domain of meaning extends
inherently into irreducible mystery, then is not meaning as
such revealed to be a self-surpassing? Is not the meaning of
transcendence revealed to be the transcendence of meaning
(subjective *and* objective genitive)?

Meaning as such grants coming-to-presence (being), allows
determinate presentment (appearance of beings), and claims
human ek-sistence for the preservation of the coming-to-presence
of what is determinately present. But mystery does not grant
itself any determinate presentment. Instead it prevails as pure
withdrawal-from-presence. Thus, in the mystery of Da-sein,
meaning reveals itself to be a transcending of itself. The
meaning of transcendence is ultimately the transcendence of
meaning.

This much was shown by the revelation of Da-sein in the
phenomenon of *Angst*. *Angst* reveals that Da-sein, the primordial
domain of meaning, also surpasses meaning. Pure Da-sein surpasses meaning *not* in the sense that it is independent of meaning, or different from meaning, but rather in the sense that
it is *more* than the articulation of world accomplished in the
linguistic grant of meaning. Pure Da-sein is more in that
precisely *as* the linguistically articulated world, Da-sein extends into pure mystery, mystery which is *non-meaning* since it
itself as such is pure *dis*-allowance of coming-to-presence.

The claim that Da-sein is not different from meaning and
yet is paradoxically more than meaning can be elaborated by
attending to the fundamental characteristics of meaning which
we introduced in Chapter II. Pure Da-sein is not different from
meaning because, in the first place, Da-sein emerges only as
the linguistic articulation of world, and in the second place,

because even as mystery, Da-sein retains the characteristics of meaning. In *Angst*, one is *claimed* by Da-sein, although *not* purposively. In this non-purposive claim, one experiences the *grant* of Da-sein's sovereign sway. And even as mystery, Da-sein remains the *allowance* of the coming-to-presence of beings, although this allowance now dissolves the otherwise compelling nature of the ordinary means-ends structure which accords to beings their ordinary *meaningfulness* (involvement in the future). Moreover, pure Da-sein first reveals the self-withholding of meaning as such from coming-to-presence. Pure Da-sein thus remains the domain of meaning, although it transcends meaning as the allowance of coming-to-presence. Meaning thus inherently surpasses itself. Meaning is the allowance of coming-to-presence, but meaning as such does not allow itself any coming-to-presence. At the heart of meaning, non-meaning, essential hiddenness in mystery, reigns supreme. Meaning as such is an irreducible transcending of the fundamental allowance of world-openness, a surpassing into the essential hiddenness and closure of mystery itself.

Little more can be said on this score except to note that this line of inquiry pushes to the very limit of understanding and reveals transcendence as such to be the *abiding finitization* of any possible understanding. Transcendence as such delivers the world *as* understanding (i.e., as *already* articulated linguistically and thus as constitutive of understanding), and yet it also essentially finitizes that world by radically refusing any culmination of the surpassing of Da-sein in some transcendental or trans-emergent (i.e., permanent, non-emergent) structure of presence. Da-sein culminates in no fixed and final structure of presence, but instead opens ever beyond fixity and structure into irreducible mystery itself. And in a very important sense, this is the final word that can be said with regard to pure Da-sein as such.

However, to acknowledge this much is not to terminate our discussion of the meaning of transcendence. We do not need to abandon our inquiry with the proclamation that transcendence as such is the surpassing of the world-extension of understanding by the irreducible mystery of Da-sein itself. To be sure, we cannot undercut this conclusion, but we can approach this

question in terms of the *special* way that transcendence as such
gives itself to be encountered in human life. This special way
is the self-allowance of mystery as mystery, the self-allowance
of the meaning of transcendence which transpires in the meaning-
domain which we shall name "the Holy."

At the outset, we must clarify what seems to be a contradiction in our remarks up to this point. We have just maintained
that transcendence as such is the surpassing of meaning as
allowance in the sense that meaning does not allow itself any
coming-to-presence. But now we are saying that the meaning-
domain of the Holy is the self-allowance of the meaning of
transcendence. How can these two claims be squared away?

The first of these claims cannot be understood to mean that
transcendence as such is beyond human encounter. To claim this
would deny the sameness of Da-sein and human ek-sistence. Instead, this claim denies that meaning as transcendent gives
itself forth in any determinate presentment after the fashion
of the coming-to-presence of beings. To use the language of the
early Heidegger, there is an "ontological difference" between
meaning as such and the beings that are allowed to come into
their particular self-appearance by virtue of the grant of meaning. And because this difference is fundamental, meaning can
allow itself to be encountered only in a different sense than
the allowing-to-come-to-presence which pertains to particular
beings. Instead of giving itself forth in this way, transcendence as meaning must allow itself to be encountered precisely
as that which withdraws from determinate presence. If this is
understood, then no contradiction is entailed in what we have
said thus far.

The Fourfold Context of the Holy

We may now return to our consideration of the Holy. In
order to discuss the meaning-domain of the Holy, we must first
discuss the way in which the Holy transpires along with other
pervasive meaning-domains. Heidegger has himself suggested a
fourfold prevailing of world, in which four meaning-domains
transpire, not as separate or independent regions of meaning,
but instead as interpenetrating aspects of the one dimension
of world-openness. Because the fundamental meaning-domains do

not stand apart from one another, we must turn to the fourfold and attempt to give some account of it, before turning to the Holy per se.

Heidegger's approach to the fourfold is by way of the holistic manner in which the particular thing shows itself forth. The initial question raised is: What is a thing? Or better still: In what does thingness, the being of the thing, consist?

It is commonly assumed that the being of a thing is either its present perceptible appearance, or else its self-supported independence. These two alternatives may be designated respectively as the idealist and the realist accounts of the being of the thing. However, there is a real question as to whether or not either of these two accounts is adequate to *how* the thing fully prevails as thing. In fact, in his remarkable essay "Das Ding" ("The Thing"), Heidegger gives a description of thingness that is dramatically at odds with either of the two traditional accounts just mentioned.

The example of the thing which Heidegger selects is a jug. For Heidegger, to inquire into the being or thingness of the jug is to seek the full, non-reduced way that the jug stands forth. If one were to attempt a description of something such as a jug, one would most likely understand such a task to be the accurate representation of the perceptual givenness of an object (Object: "That which stands over against," as in the German *Gegenstand*), or of the object's substantial self-subsistence. In the one case one would undertake to describe the jug in terms of the perceptual properties of its sides and bottom, the color and texture of their surfaces, as well as their thickness and mass, other properties such as brittleness, combustibility, etc., type and number of decorative features, and so on. Or, in the other case, one would attempt to describe the jug in terms of the nature of the material out of which it has been formed, whether this account be in terms of some metaphysical understanding of substance, or in terms of modern scientific notions of organic, chemical, molecular, atomic, and sub-atomic levels of composition. But in either case, Heidegger considers such accounts, however complete on their own terms, to be essentially *abstract*, simply because a jug does not occur in its fullness either as a perceptual givenness or as a particular constellation of self-subsistent material.

How, then, does the jug occur in its fullness? The initial
and deceptively simple answer to this question is that the jug
occurs primarily as a vessel, and not a mere object. This
means that to the being of the jug belongs its capacity to hold.
This capacity to hold is the key to Heidegger's description of
the being of the jug. Accordingly, Heidegger asks the following
question: Is it the materiality of the jug, the impermeability
of its sides and bottom, which first creates the possibility
of its holding something? Is the vessel-character of the jug a
merely secondary characteristic of the jug, one that is derivative from the presumably primary fact of the jug's materiality--
its solidity, its closed configuration, its impermeability?
Or, is it the other way around, such that the materiality of the
jug is itself in some sense determined by the prior requirements
of its vessel-character?

To answer these questions, one must inquire phenomenologically into the essence of holding itself. This Heidegger does,
with the result that it is not the sides and bottom of the jug
which are discovered to accomplish and thus to ground the holding, but rather the holding is possible because of the *emptiness*
between the sides and over the bottom. It is this emptiness,
this void, which itself first allows the possibility that something like holding may take place.

> When we fill the jug with wine, do we pour the wine
> into the sides and bottom? At most, we pour the wine
> between the sides and over the bottom. Sides and
> bottom are, to be sure, what is impermeable in the
> vessel. But what is impermeable is not yet what
> does the holding. When we fill the jug, the pour-
> ing that fills it flows into the empty jug. This
> emptiness or void [*die Leere*] is what does the
> vessel's holding. This void, this nothingness
> in the jug, is what the jug is as the holding
> vessel.[1]

The importance of this description, if it be accepted, is that
the being of the jug cannot be understood simply in terms of
its material givenness. Instead, one is impelled to accept the
radical conclusion that the thingness of the jug is to be found
in the empty void that allows holding to take place.

The import of this conclusion for our purposes is that
this description of the jug's thingness or being reveals that
things are not, when considered radically, internal

self-samenesses (whether perceptual or substantival) that can
be grasped in categorial or representational description. A
categorial description can either grasp the jug idealistically,
i.e., in terms of its perceptual givenness, or realistically,
i.e., in terms of the substance which gives it internal self-
subsistence. But such descriptions can never confront the jug
as a vessel whose basic character is *to hold*; they can never
confront the jug *as jug*. Heidegger's case here rests on the
phenomenological claim that the vessel-character of the jug
has primacy over the material givenness of the jug-object. In
turn, this entails that the void which holds pertains more to
the being of the jug than do the jug's *actual* sides and bottom.

But how can one speak of an emptiness or void as pertaining
to the being of the jug? And how is it that such a void is
deemed to be more fundamental than the actual materiality of
the jug-object? To answer this, one must first recognize that
material impermeability itself is not sufficient to ground the
possibility that holding take place. This is because the holding takes place *outside* the internally self-contained material
structure of the jug-object. If one simply thinks of the jug-
object in terms of the internal self-identity of its sides and
bottom, one is forced to admit that this self-identity on its
own terms does not make allowance for anything such as holding
to occur. The sides and bottom simply are solid, continuous,
etc. But no such categorial property is *itself* the allowance
of holding, or the ground of such a possibility. Thus, the
remarkable conclusion must be adhered to that the sides and
bottom of themselves *do not hold*. Holding as a possibility must
stem from elsewhere.

As we have seen, Heidegger's phenomenological account is
that holding is allowed by the emptiness that prevails between
the sides and over the bottom. Thus, the impermeability of the
jug with respect to holding is itself allowed for by this more
primordial emptiness. The very possibility that there be such
a material feature as impermeability is itself founded in the
primordial prevalence of emptiness which grants the possibilities
of holding, containing, preserving.

How, then, is this emptiness to be understood? Since
emptiness is more primordial than the given materiality of the

jug-object's sides and bottom, the jug's emptiness cannot be
understood in terms of the fixed delineations of those sides
and bottom. The jug's emptiness is not *confined* to the actual
spatio-temporal nexus which is defined by the material givenness
of the jug-object. Instead, this emptiness pervades the entire
realm within which the jug as material object may occur. The
jug's primordial emptiness is not restricted by the materiality
of the jug, but instead the jug as material object is a
reduction to specific actuality of the primordial being of the
jug, i.e., of the emptiness which founds holding, containing,
preserving.

     What is being said here is that the being of the jug is
not restricted to the actual determinate configuration of the
jug-object because it *pervades the entire world* in which the
jug can be manifest itself in its particular determinateness.
The emptiness which first allows holding to take place, and
which is thus the jug's emptiness, is nevertheless a feature
of the world as such. It is an articulation of world. It is
a meaning-allowance which first grants the possibility that the
jug-object can meaningfully emerge within human awareness.

     We can now see that this exposition of the being of the
jug ties together many of the themes which we have already
discussed in earlier sections of this work. In discussing the
jug's being as emptiness, we have moved from the ontic particularity of the jug to the underlying meaning-allowance which
transcends both the objectivity of the jug (its internal self-
sameness) and its subjective appearance for consciousness. Thus,
since we have moved from the ontic particularity of the jug to
the meaning of the jug, we can see exemplified here our earlier
characterization of meaning-as-such as allowance, grant and
claim. Emptiness is allowance in that it is what first allows
holding to take place, and thus it first allows the jug to come
forth as vessel, as jug. In addition, we can also see that this
meaning-allowance is a grant that precedes all human endeavor,
all human volition and control. We say this because emptiness
grants itself as the founding possibility of the jug as jug,
whereas human activity has influence and control only over the
jug-object (things in their particularity). Volition is thus
relative to the particular things which can be manipulated

through some mode of exertion. But there is no such influence which obtains in relation to the meaning-allowances which grant the possibilities of things in their particularities. Emptiness is thus the meaning-grant of the possibility of holding, a grant which is preserved in the pre-volitional receptivity of human ek-sistence.

And finally, we can understand emptiness as claim insofar as emptiness prevails *only* as that which claims the openness of Da-sein for its own grant of the possibility of the jug as vessel. It is only within the ecstatic dwelling of ek-sistence that the grant of emptiness can prevail. Thus, human awareness as claimed by the meaning-grant of emptiness is essential for that grant to hold sway as allowance, as an articulation of world.

We may now return to Heidegger's inquiry into the being of the jug, and ask with him how it is that emptiness prevails as an articulation of world. The question that Heidegger raises at this point is whether or not scientific representation of any kind can reveal the character of the jug's emptiness.[2] His answer is that it cannot, because science can only encounter emptiness in terms of its strict attunement to actuality. Accordingly, emptiness for science can only be represented as the *lack* of actuality, i.e., as vacuum. However, the phenomenon of emptiness reveals itself to be *other* than any mere vacuum if we allow this phenomenon to manifest itself on its own terms. And to allow it to manifest itself on its own terms means to attend to emptiness, not as the absence of actuality but rather as meaning.

If we now recall a claim that we advanced in Chapter II, namely that meaning is always linguistic, i.e., conveyed in the dialectic of language, then we can say the following: To attend to the phenomenon of emptiness on its own terms is to attend to its linguistic conveyance. In harmony with this conclusion, Heidegger turns next, in the essay we are considering, directly to the language which is related to holding. This language is summarized in the following passage:

> How does the emptiness of the jug hold? It holds
> by taking what is poured in. It holds by keeping
> and retaining what it took in. The emptiness
> holds in a twofold manner: taking and keeping.

> The word "hold" is therefore ambiguous. Neverthe-
> less, the taking of what is poured in and the keeping
> of what was poured belong together. But their unity
> is determined by the outpouring for which the jug
> is fitted as a jug. The twofold holding of the
> emptiness rests on the outpouring....To pour from
> the jug is to give. The holding of the vessel
> occurs in the giving of the outpouring....The
> giving, whereby the jug is a jug, gathers in the
> twofold holding--in the outpouring....The jug's
> jug-character consists in the poured gift of the
> pouring out.[3]

What we see in this passage is Heidegger's attempt to follow
responsively in thought the interinvolvement of the complex
meaning-relations which are "gathered" in the meaning of "hold."
In this way, he hopes to ek-sist in thought throughout the world-
articulation that "centers," or is nodally gathered, in the
essential character of the jug.

What one finds in this kind of thinking in response to the
meaning-relations that are gathered in the jug's holding is that
pattern of meaning-relations that includes taking, keeping, and
pouring out as gift. Furthermore, one discovers that pouring-
out is primary in the sense that only because the meaning-allowance of pouring out as gift prevails can there also be the
meaning-possibilities of taking and keeping. The meaning of
taking and keeping depends upon the more primordial meaning of
pouring out as gift.

The next step that Heidegger takes in his attempt to follow
in thought the articulation of world that is centered in the
being of the jug is to attend to the fullness of the meaning-
allowance which he has named "pouring out as gift." And what
Heidegger discovers at this point is a gathering in this meaning-
allowance of the most pervasive meaning-domains of world-openness,
meaning-domains which nevertheless held in the unity of their
mutual interinvolvement by the gathered unity of "pouring out as
gift." These fundamental meaning-domains are fourfold, and yet
they are the oneness of the articulated world. In the following
passage, Heidegger names the four fundamental domains of world-
openness, and also discloses how they are gathered into their
oneness in the meaning-allowance of outpouring.

> In the gift of the outpouring that is drink, mortals
> abide [*weilen*] in their own way. In the gift of the
> outpouring that is a libation, the divinities abide

> in their own way, they who receive back the gift
> of the giving as the gift of the donation. In
> the gift of the outpouring, mortals and divinities
> each dwell in their different ways. Earth and sky
> dwell in the gift of the outpouring. In the gift
> of the outpouring earth and sky, divinities and
> mortals dwell *together all at once*. These four,
> united by and from themselves, belong together.
> Preceding everything that is present, they are
> enfolded into a single fourfold.[4]

What Heidegger is saying here is that in the tissue of meaning-
relatedness that allows the coming-to-presence of the jug as
jug, there is collected into the singular world-context of that
coming-to-presence the four interpenetrating meaning-domains in
which human beings are given to ek-sist. These four interpenetrating meaning-domains are the earth, the sky, divinities and
mortals.

To speak of earth as a fundamental meaning-domain is to
speak of the self-enclosing aspect of all coming-to-presence,
the impenetrable rock-like foundation of givenness which both
shelters and bears forth the fruits of presence. Earth is the
allowance of tangibility, in whose dull opacity meaning is
sheltered, and in whose bearing of all coming-forth, meaning
issues into concrete presence. Earth sustains presence, as the
"ground" from which and in terms of which all that comes forth
takes its stand.[5]

To speak of sky as a fundamental meaning-domain is to contrast to earth the open reaches of the heavens, the expensive-
ness of that openness, into whose unbounded extent we are
beckoned to stretch ourselves by the paradoxical *closeness* of
those ever distant beacons, the moon, the sun, the stars. The
sky is the domain of openness, of future, and hence of the
destined yet undetermined paths that history will take. Standing on earth we are beckoned, invited to traverse the open paths
of the sky. Because sky prevails, our world is not closed, not
simply determinate, not granite-like, but is open, expansive,
futural, inviting, reaching ever outward into the destined
unknown.

To speak of divinities as a fundamental meaning-domain is
to speak of the extraordinary occurrences of meaning, those
dawning encounters in which our mundane, culturally encrusted
sense of reality is broken by an impingement from beyond the

ordinary, by an overabundance of compelling claim, by an encap-
turing draft of one's being that cannot be circumscribed, brought
into particularization, or circumvented. Although Heidegger
speaks of "divinities" [Göttlichen] in this connection, presumably to emphasize the occasional character of such encounters,
we propose instead to speak of the Holy, in order to emphasize
the singularity of this meaning-domain, even though it does not
prevail continuously in our immediate neighborhood of meaning.
We will, of course, have more to say concerning this meaning-
domain of the Holy, inasmuch as it is this meaning-domain which
provides the special "place" where meaning as such gives itself
to be encountered as transcendent. But before extending our
discussion of this meaning-domain, we need to complete our
exposition of the fourfold of meaning by mentioning the last of
the four meaning-domains, the mortals, and then by saying something about the oneness of the fourfold.

To speak of mortals as a fundamental meaning-domain is to
speak of the pervasive individualization unto death which characterizes all ek-sistent habitation and preservation of world.
Along with the sheltering and nurturing self-enclosure of earth,
the open expansiveness of historical destiny in sky, the compelling, non-circumscribable claim of the divinities in the Holy,
there is also the pervasive prevailing of Death. By "Death,"
one is not at all here speaking merely of the objectifiable
occurrence of organic demise, the specific cessation of life-
functions in one particular organism. Instead, one is speaking
phenomenologically of the pervasive shroud that hangs over all
awareness, and hence over fundamental world-openness itself.

> Death is the encasement of Nothing, that is of
> that which in every respect is never something
> that merely is, but which nevertheless prevails,
> indeed as the mystery of being itself. As the
> encasement of Nothing, Death shelters within
> itself the prevailing of Being. As the encasement
> of Nothing, Death is the shelter of Being.[6]

In this passage, Heidegger says that Death is the sheltering
shroud which refuses any culmination of coming-to-presence in
absolute presence, but instead withholds presence and thus
preserves primordial mystery. In addition, death is that which
finitizes Dasein. Death encompasses and utterly permeates all

coming-to-presence. Death prevails at the heart of the fourfold, and only because Death is already holding sway is there
life, concrete experience, possibility, movement, and indeed
the eternity of the moment which stops the tensive rush of time.
Because Death prevails, there is no absolute culmination of
presence in utter and lifeless self-completion. Instead, there
is culmination only in the sway of Death, within pervasive
deathliness. Coming-to-presence cannot finally be thought except as it is embraced by Death.

We have now spoken of the four fundamental domains of meaning into which world-openness is articulated in the grant of
language. But these four domains are not discrete regions,
somehow abiding apart from each other. Instead, they occur only
insofar as they mirror each other, and thus totally interpene-
trate each other.

> Earth and sky, divinities and mortals--at one with
> one another of their own accord--belong together
> by way of the oneness of the united fourfold. Each
> of the four mirrors in its own way the prevailing
> of the others. Each thereby reflects itself in
> its own way into its own within the oneness of
> the four. This mirroring is not the presentation
> of a likeness. The mirroring, clearing [*lichtend*]
> each of the four, appropriates their own prevailing
> into simple belonging to each other.[7]

Earth does not prevail except as it bears forth into the sky's
openness, and reaches toward the non-traversible land of the
divinities within the shroud of death. And sky does not prevail
except as it expands in strife with the earth's nurturing self-
enclosure, joining forces with the non-circumventible claim of
the divinities (yet offering no path into the Holy as such),
and presenting its unboundedness as an offering before the
shrine of Death's overpowering finitization. And the Holy does
not prevail except as it appropriates the neutral unboundedness
of the sky into its own compelling claim, standing ever beyond
and yet reaching down to touch the earth, addressing the mortals
who are thereby drafted by the Holy into the non-surpassable
rule of their own death. And Death itself does not prevail
except as it emerges in the other three as the irreducible
threat of non-presence, the threat of the collapse of sky, of
the utter hiddenness of earth, and of the mortal's loss of
world-dwelling. There is thus a oneness to this fourfold, a

singularity in which there is multiplicity only insofar as the
four domains transpire in their "mirror-play," in their mutual
appropriation of each other.

Now that we have discussed the fourfold of meaning, we
may now return to our discussion of the Holy. As we have said,
the Holy is that meaning-domain within the fourfold which allows
the divinities to show forth. And the divinities are those
special encounters in which human ek-sistence experiences itself
to be drafted into a claim that surpasses the kind of claim
that one ordinarily confronts in one's everyday life.

In everyday life, one experiences other beings as in one
way or another laying claim to one's attention. The ordinary
awareness of anything thus always includes some *demand*, even if
it be merely the demand to observe, to pay attention to what is
there.[8] In Chapter II, we have maintained that laying claim to
human ek-sistence (awareness) is a basic feature of meaning as
such. In light of that conclusion, we may now say that beings
themselves as merely particular beings do not lay claim upon
us. However, the *being* of a being, which itself is the gathered
meaning-articulation of world in that being (recall the jug
example) is the source of that being's claim. Insofar as beings
confront us in the gathered world-context of meaning-relatedness,
they lay claim upon us.[9]

The way in which beings ordinarily lay claim upon us is
relative and thus circumventible. It is relative in the sense
that the ordinary claim of a being is contingent upon its placement within some strand of purposiveness. Beings claim us relative to their projected part in the accomplishment of some
purpose or end, even if that end be merely to observe purely,
knowledge *for the sake of* knowledge. But the relativity of
claim as it is ordinarily experienced entails that for the claim
to be effective, the purpose that sustains the claim must be
appropriated as one's own. One must ek-sist tensively into that
purpose's futurity in order for the claim to make itself felt.

Tensive ek-sistence into the futurity of purpose, however,
is not a given of human being. Our previous discussion of *Angst*
led us to the conclusion that in *Angst*, pure Da-sein is revealed
to be purposeless, devoid of any means-end structure, and thus
to be the self-surpassing of meaning. But human ek-sistence

inherits Da-sein itself as its essential preserve. Accordingly, human being is at base essentially free to escape the tensive projection into purposiveness, a projection which results from the interinvolvements of beings that are provided in meaning-allowance. And this is to say that human being is essentially free from the ordinary claims of beings, of whatever is in particular. Human being is not fundamentally prey to this manner of claim.

In contrast to the claims which ordinary beings impose upon us, the claims which are encountered as divinities do not occur in the context of relative purpose and thus are not in principle circumventible. The claim of a divinity is both absolute for as long as it holds sway, and inherently inescapable. One experiences such a claim not in relation to some future accomplishment or projection, but as a fully occurrent claim, one that does not refract itself into future projection. Instead, such a claim is all consuming in the occurrent encounter. It is dyadic (the individual overwhelmed by divine claim), rather than triadic (the individual experiencing the claim of something relative to some tissue of purposive interinvolvement). Accordingly, human ek-sistence cannot stand apart from the claim of divinity as it can from the claims of mundane beings. The being (ek-sistence) of human being is *totally* claimed by divinity for the divinity's draft, or address, and thus the divinity, unlike mundane beings, is the "measure" against which man must measure himself.[10]

The Holy is that meaning-domain within the fourfold which allows the unsurpassable overwhelmingness of claim as such to prevail. In addition, it is of the essence of meaning as claim to institute the very structure of human awareness and thus to overwhelm human being.[11] Human awareness is essentially over-whelmed by meaning as claim because, as we have seen, there is no human "essence" prior to the ek-sistent reception of the emergent grant of meaning. But in light of this, it can now be said that the Holy is the "place" where meaning as such in its character of overwhelming uncircumventibility is itself given forth to be encountered as such. Only as divinity is meaning encountered as transcendent, i.e., surpassing the determinate, relative, and hence limited (circumventible) claims of ordinary

beings. The divinities emerge in their surpassing of the scope
of ordinary claim. And in this surpassing, this transcendence,
man is himself measured, for it is only in the encounter with
divinity that man experiences the full extent of the utterly
prevolitional receptivity of his ecstatic ek-sistence. In the
transcendence of meaning as encountered in the divinities, man
receives his fundamental and essential measure.[12]

All that remains to be said in this connection is that *how*
the divinity encounters man is what determines man's measure.
Meaning as transcendence is emergent in the divinities, and *how*
meaning emerges is the establishment of transcendence. Transcendence is thus to be encountered and understood by man *only* in
encounter with divinity. There is no other path to an understanding of transcendence, for there "is" no transcendence except
as transcendence prevails in its self-giving in the emergent
divinities. Transcendence prevails in its self-giving in the
emergent divinities. Transcendence prevails, and man is accorded
his essential measure, only so long as the divinities encounter
man with the claim of transcendence.

The Danger Threatening the Prevailing of the Fourfold

If we were to continue the present line of discussion
uninterrupted, the next step would be to attempt to give voice
to the way in which we are now claimed for transcendence by emergent divinity. In order to do this, we would need to pass beyond
the term "transcendence" itself, insofar as it suggests a fixed
or trans-emergent claim, and attend solely to the way in which
we are now called forth and given measure by the emergent
appropriation of the divinity. However, we cannot move directly
to this next step. This cannot be done because the path for
such an advance is not now cleared. Instead, our ek-sistent
habitation of world is confronted with a reigning danger which
threatens the very emergence of a divinely instituted measure
of human being, and hence of transcendence itself. This danger
threatens to nihilate the human occupation of world-openness
itself as measured in the divine draft of ek-sistence. What
is this danger, and how does it transpire?

Heidegger himself has broached the question of this fundamental danger threatening Da-sein in several of his essays.[13]
In these essays, Heidegger takes account of the danger and
suggests how the danger is itself overcome. We need now to
pursue the thinking of these essays, if we hope to advance our
inquiry into transcendence, now thought in terms of emergent
divinity as the measure of human ek-sistence.

We have stressed earlier that Da-sein, primordial relatedness, does not eventuate in a trans-emergent structure of
presence, but rather prevails as the holding open of world which
is itself a withholding from presence in irreducible mystery.
If we take this point seriously, then we must understand that
the meaning of transcendence can be sought and encountered as
claim only within the occurrent emergence of divinity and the
measure of human ek-sistence that is instituted therein. But
does the emergence of divinity now characterize the world
articulation that is given as our essential preserve? Is the
world that is now granted for ek-sistent dwelling a realm in
which the Holy prevails and divinities (or the divinity) come
forth to draft human being? How is the world now open, and
what possibilities of awareness are emergent therein?[14]

In the essay "Der Satz der Identität," Heidegger directly
raises this question. In Chapter III, we pursued the thinking
of this essay up to the point at which it is stated that the
belonging of man and being can be genuinely experienced only in
a "leap" that springs away from being, considered apart from
its relatedness to man, and from man, considered apart from its
relatedness to being. And we said that from within the horizon
of metaphysical, representational thinking, the belongingness
(Da-sein) into which the leap springs can only be termed an
abyss.[15] With this suggestion, we then turned away from this
essay to attend to Heidegger's earlier discussion of the Nothing
and primordial mystery that is found in the essay "Was Ist
Metaphysik?"

We must now return to the line of thinking that is found
in "Der Satz der Identität." As we have said, Heidegger raises
the question as to how the world is now open for human dwelling.
He asks: In what "constellation" of being and man do we now
find ourselves?[16] The answer to this question, he then says,

seems readily available. The world, the "constellation" of
being and man, in which we now find ourselves, is the world of
technology.[17]

In what sense can it be said that technology characterizes
Da-sein's primordial relatedness? To be sure, technology in
the usual sense of the term is not the way that ek-sistent holding open of world transpires, but is instead a particular set
of implements, techniques, items of information, commercial
and social complexes, projects, etc., which occur *within* the
world and seemingly *under* the control of man. How, then, can
technology be understood as the way that Da-sein as such now
transpires?

To distinguish between technology in the usual sense and
what he wishes to attend to, Heidegger begins to speak of the
"essence" (*Wesen*: "prevailing," "perduring"[18]) of technology.
In other words, he suggests that the pervasive *way* in which
everything is given in a technological context, and hence the
way that technology itself endures, is the constellation of
man and being in which we now find ourselves. Da-sein now
occurs as the reign of the *essence* of technology.

The essence of technology is itself nothing technological.[19]
The essence of technology is nothing at the disposal of man,
but is instead a grant of meaning. As meaning, it is also both
claim and allowance, as well as a self-withholding. In keeping
with our understanding of allowance as a primary characteristic
of meaning, we may now ask concerning the essence of technology:
what is it that is allowed in this articulation of world?

The allowance that occurs as the essence of technology is
the way that beings are allowed to come-to-presence under its
sway. It is the way that beings are revealed. Concerning the
revealing that rules throughout modern technology, Heidegger
says: "[This revealing] has the character of a setting-upon
[*stellen*] in the sense of a challenging-forth."[20] That which
is revealed under the sway of the essence of technology is that
which is available for a setting-upon that challenges forth.
Beings are revealed as already subject to challenge, a challenge
that demands of whatever is revealed that it yield to challenge,
that it be available for such a challenge and subject to such
challenge. What is the character of this challenge? How are

beings allowed to come-to-presence under the reign of this
challenging-forth?

> What kind of unconcealment, then, is characteristic
> of that which comes to stand through the setting-
> upon that challenges forth? Everywhere, everything
> is disposed [*bestellt*] to stand in place and in
> order [*auf der Stelle zur Stelle zu stehen*], and
> indeed to stand in disposability for a further
> ordering. Whatever is thus disposed has its own
> stand. We call it the standing-reserve [*Bestand*].[21]

Under the sway of the essence of technology, beings are allowed
to come-to-presence only as that which is disposed to be set in
order, as that which is subject to order and is thus subordinated
to structure. Under such a meaning-allowance, beings are present
as *instances*, as mere substitutes within a structure of coher-
ence. As standing-reserve, the coming-to-presence (being) of
beings is no longer the gathering of the world's prevailing
meaning-domains (cf. the jug example, pp. 106-112 above), but
is rather the mere *incidence* of the particular that is subjugated
to the structure of some order. Under this subjugation, one
being may substitute completely for another being. One particular being can thus be *replaced* by another and nothing is lost,
for the structure, the order remains firm. The being of beings
under the sway of the essence of technology is thus *the incidental, incidentality*. As incidental, a being is completely
given over to its disposability to be ordered, to be subjected
to calculation, to planning, and ultimately to the manipulation
which takes place as technology in the usual sense of the term.[22]

We have been speaking of the essence of technology as a
meaning-allowance and have seen that the allowance can be characterized as standing-reserve. The essence of technology is
also a meaning-grant. Heidegger himself acknowledges this when
he says the following:

> The essence of modern technology sets man upon the
> way of that revealing through which the actual
> everywhere, more or less distinctly, is brought
> into standing-reserve. "To set upon a way" means
> "to send" [*schicken*] in our ordinary language.
> We name that gathering sending which first sets
> man upon a way of revealing--destiny [*das Geschick*].
> It is from this destiny that the essence of all
> history [*Geschichte*] is determined.[23]

Thus the essence of technology, as a way of revealing (i.e., a
meaning-allowance) is also a "destiny" that sets man upon the
way of such meaning-allowance. It is thus an emergent grant of
meaning which human beings receive but do not control.

In addition, Heidegger also speaks of the essence of
technology as claim. The challenge that besets being in the
sway of the essence of technology demands that beings come-to-
presence only as standing-reserve. But man also is subjected
to this challenge in that he is claimed for the ek-sistent
securing of standing-reserve. "To the same degree that being
is challenged, man also is challenged, that is to say, engaged
[gestellt] to secure all beings, with which he has something to
do, as the standing-reserve for his planning and calculating,
and to carry this disposing [Bestellen] on past all bounds."[24]
As such a claim that challenges both being as such and man as
such, the essence of technology is a gathering, not of the
fourfold into the mirror-play of its four meaning-domains, but
rather a gathering of man's dwelling in world-openness into the
ordering of everything, a gathering of human ek-sistence into
the preservation of standing-reserve. As a claim that gathers
man and being in this way, Heidegger names the essence of
technology the "gathering-into-orderability" [Ge-Stell].[25]

If gathering-into-orderability is thought as such, i.e.,
as meaning-allowance, then it is received as the emergent destiny
as which Da-sein is now occurring. As such, gathering-into-
orderability is not the danger threatening Da-sein. However,
Heidegger's own thinking pursuit of Da-sein was confronted
time after time with the elusiveness of Da-sein as such. Da-
sein, the ultimate field of meaning, is never present as itself
because, as we have said on several occasions, the openness of
world never itself attains to a standing structure of self-
presentation. Instead, its fundamental character is withdrawal
from presence, i.e., essential mystery.

The import of this fundamental character of Da-sein for
our present consideration of gathering-into-orderability is
that this destiny cannot be thought of as a standing structure
of presence that one can attend to as such (e.g., in some sort
of transcendental "reduction" of consciousness). Instead,
gathering-into-orderability is itself fundamentally characterized

by withdrawal from presence, as is all meaning as such. The way
that this characteristic of meaning as such prevails in gathering-into-orderability is what constitutes the present danger to
the ek-sistent preservation of the fourfold of world-openness.

Danger prevails not because gathering-into-orderability
as such prevails, but because gathering-into-orderability is not
encountered *as such* and thus does *not* prevail. This is to say
that the danger emerges precisely insofar as gathering-into-
orderability is not experienced on its own terms as meaning-
allowance, meaning-grant and meaning-claim, but instead falls
into oblivion under the pervasive illusion that human will is
the master of all things technological. It is because we do
not experience the world-gathering of gathering-into-orderability
as the meaning-allowance whose foundational self-granting claims
human ek-sistence for its own that prevailing Da-sein is
threatened with a truly radical danger. Heidegger expresses
this point in terms of meaning-as-claim when he says:

> Man stands so decisively *in the consequences* of
> the challenging-forth of gathering-into-ordera-
> ability that he is not aware of gathering-into-
> orderability as a claim, fails to see himself as
> the one who is claimed, and thus also fails in
> every way to be aware of the way that he ek-sists
> in terms of his own enduring [*aus seinem Wesen*]
> in the domain of an exhortation....26

It is because man stands in the *consequences* of gathering-into-
orderability that he does not experience gathering-into-orderability as such. Man stands in the volitional accomplishments
of the technological world, and sees himself as the ultimate
master of that world. But these accomplishments, and this
presumed mastery, are themselves dependent upon the pervasive
collecting of world into order that is gathering-into-orderability. Gathering-into-orderability prevails by gathering
everything into the placement that is at the disposal of human
calculation and hence of manipulation. Man himself is gathered
into such placement to the extent that his ek-sistence is fully
handed over to the calculating, the ordering, and finally the
manipulating that characterizes the technological world. But
the paradox in this is that precisely to the extent that man is
claimed by gathering-into-orderability and lives out the
challenge of gathering-into-orderability, this destiny as such

is lost. In its very overwhelming triumph over human being,
the meaning of gathering-into-orderability as allowance, as
grant, as claim withdraws and thus is lost.

This, then, is the danger, that the way that Da-sein as
gathering-into-orderability prevails is itself a disguising of
itself, a falling-into-oblivion precisely in and through its
own triumph.

> The prevailing [*Wesen*] of gathering-into-orderability
> is that setting-upon gathered into itself which way-
> lays the truth of its own prevailing with oblivion
> [*Vergessenheit*]. This waylaying disguises itself,
> in that it develops into the setting in order of
> everything that presences as standing-reserve, estab-
> lishes itself in the standing-reserve, and rules as
> the standing-reserve. Gathering-into-orderability
> prevails as the danger. But does the danger there-
> with announce itself *as* danger? No. To be sure,
> men are at all times and in all places exceedingly
> oppressed by dangers and exigencies. But *the*
> danger, namely being itself endangering itself in
> the truth of its prevailing, remains veiled and
> disguised. *This disguising is what is most dangerous
> in the danger.*27

The prevailing of gathering-into-orderability is thus thoroughly
paradoxical, in that its triumph is at the same time its own
oblivion. Gathering-into-orderability rules only insofar as it
fails to hold sway as such and instead *exhausts itself* in the
total entrapment of everything in standing-reserve, i.e., in
orderability. This paradoxical self-exhaustion of gathering-
into-orderability in the total triumph of its own allowance of
standing-reserve is thus the danger, inherent in the prevailing
of gathering-into-orderability, which threatens Da-sein itself.

The point has now been reached from which the question of
the danger's relation to the fourfold may now be raised.
Initially, it would seem as though one can glean two *different*
characterizations of the way that emergent Da-sein is transpiring from Heidegger's writings. On the one hand, he has characterized emergent Da-sein as the fourfold prevailing of meaning.
On the other hand, he also seems to suggest that emergent Da-sein
is now transpiring as the triumph of gathering-into-orderability
which is the danger. Which of these characterizations are we
to accept? Or, do we need to choose between them? Are they
mutually exclusive, or do they both belong together in one more
encompassing characterization?

What we wish to suggest is that these two characterizations
of emergent Da-sein are neither mutually exclusive, nor are they
to be brought together in a characterization that somehow
harmonizes them both. In the first place, it is not necessary
that we choose between the fourfold and the danger, as if one
characterization were correct and the other in error. Instead,
it may be that *both* are correct, that both accurately characterize the way that Da-sein now transpires.

However, this is not to suggest that these two characterizations can be harmonized. On the contrary, it may be that there
is an essential *strife* between these two characterizations.
Perhaps Da-sein does not simply transpire in accord with one or
the other of these two characterizations, but is rather itself
in strife with itself, emerging on the whole as the triumph of
gathering-into-orderability in the oblivion of meaning as such,
and yet flashing now and then as the fourfold realm of transcendent meaning.[28]

If this is indeed correct, if Da-sein itself is transpiring
as a fundamental conflict between the fourfold and the danger
inherent in the triumph of gathering-into-orderability, then
this triumph in its own oblivion is not absolute. The triumph
reigns supreme whenever human beings are totally handed over to
orderability, and thus experience themselves *only* as centers of
volition at whose disposal and for whose calculations everything
(including, paradoxically, God and the gods) is set out. For
the most part, this is indeed how we experience ourselves. Whatever is, whether familiar or strange, discovered or still yet-
to-be-discovered, is by and large already pre-cast as subject at
least to the disposition of the human intellect, and hence to
the order whose shifting yet relatively fixed structure is
itself *constitutive* of conceptual intellection. And yet, we do
not all of us at all times experience ourselves in the supremacy
of calculability. Rarely, but nevertheless unmistakably, Da-sein
flashes not as the supremacy of calculability but instead as
the realm of meaning as such, as the incomparable reign of
transcendent allowance, grant, and claim.

The danger is thus not absolute. It is the radical danger
threatening Da-sein itself, and yet the *threat* is not the utter
annihilation of Da-sein but rather the way that Da-sein threatens

itself in its inherent and irreducible withholding-from-presence.
Da-sein threatens itself with its own oblivion, and yet in this
very threat *as threat*, Da-sein itself prevails. And it is in
this paradoxical twist that Heidegger sees the possibility of a
saving which saves Da-sein as such from its own threatening
oblivion, and thus holds open the possibility that human ek-
sistence may experience itself in the transcendent measure that
is meted out in the claim of divinity as this emerges in the
mirror-play of the Holy within the fourfold.

The Saving of Da-sein in
Bringing-into-Ownness

For Da-sein to withstand its own danger, for it to counter-
prevail in the face of its own oblivion, the danger must not be
forgotten but must itself be *preserved* in ek-sistence *as danger*.
For the most part, Da-sein now transpires as gathering-into-
orderability, which, we have seen, is itself a pervasive meaning-
context in the sense of meaning-allowance, meaning-grant, and
meaning claim. Thus, when gathering-into-orderability is preserved in human ek-sistence *as* gathering-into-orderability, it
is preserved as a destiny of meaning. However, the allowance
of gathering-into-orderability is precisely such as to dis-allow
such preservation. Gathering-into-orderability is thus paradoxical in that it triumphs in its own oblivion, when ek-sistence
is drafted totally and without remainder into the hegemonistic
claim of orderability and disposability for volitional pursuits.
In light of this, Da-sein as gathering-into-orderability can
prevail *as danger* only when Da-sein counter-prevails against the
triumph of the oblivion inherent in the allowance of gathering-
into-orderability, only when Da-sein strives against itself as
gathering-into-orderability and discloses itself as the danger
of oblivion inherent in gathering-into-orderability.

Does Da-sein strive against itself in this manner? Is there
a counter-prevailing of Da-sein against its own triumph in the
oblivion of gathering-into-orderability? Does Da-sein emerge
as such a primordial conflict, and is human ek-sistence thereby
drafted into the needful preservation of such conflict?

It is not hyperbole to say that Heidegger's entire life's
work is predicated upon the claim that Da-sein does transpire

as primordial strife, as a counter-prevailing that checks the
absolute triumph of its own destiny in the oblivion of gathering-into-orderability. Heidegger's lifelong pursuit of the
meaning of being, and his distinction of the truth of being from
the truth of beings, rests upon his phenomenological claim that
Da-sein does at rare times (e.g., in poetic "inspiration") strive
against its own destined oblivion, and thereby stand disclosed
as Da-sein, i.e., as non-volitional, non-orderable, "transcendent"[29] meaning-context. Da-sein flashes as itself on these
rare occasions, and thereby comes into its own truth. The truth
of being, the disclosing of primordial relatedness as such,
thereby transpires.

How can we give thought to Da-sein's counter-prevailing
striving against its own destined oblivion in the triumph of
gathering-into-orderability? The first step for the thinker to
take is to attend to the oblivion *as such*, and thereby to become
aware of the already prevailing oblivion as the radical danger
that it is. If the danger comes to light expressly as the danger
that it is, then perhaps, says Heidegger, Da-sein may "turn"
from its own oblivion and turn into its own truth, i.e., turn
homeward and *as* Da-sein flash within the totality of orderable
beings.[30]

This "flashing" of Da-sein, this "turning-in" in which the
danger expressly transpires as danger, is the safekeeping of the
truth, the disclosedness of being itself. It is the coming-into-
its-own of Da-sein as such.

> When, accordingly, the danger is as the danger,
> then the waylaying that is the way being itself
> waylays its truth with oblivion expressly comes
> into its own and transpires [*ereignet*]. When
> this *waylaying-with-oblivion* does expressly come
> into its own, then oblivion as such turns in and
> abides. Thus rescued through this abiding from
> falling away out of remembrance, it is no longer
> oblivion. With such in-turning, the oblivion
> relating to being's safekeeping is no longer the
> oblivion of being. When the danger is as the
> danger with the turning about of oblivion, the
> safekeeping of being transpires by coming into
> its own; world transpires by coming into its own.[31]

In this passage, Heidegger uses a verb that names the counter-
prevailing striving of Da-sein against its own destined oblivion
in the triumph of gathering-into-orderability, and thus that

names the in-turning of Da-sein as it flashes in its own disclosedness and brings to pass the truth of being itself. This
verb is the German *sich ereignen*. We have translated this verb
with the phrase: "to transpire by coming into its own." In
this verb, and in the noun derived from it, namely *Ereignis*,
we come to the heart of the simplicity of Heidegger's thought,
the simple flashing of the mystery of Da-sein as such.

The verb *sich ereignen* in ordinary German means "to happen,
to occur, to come to pass." But Heidegger penetrates beyond
this ordinary sense to the center of the word's meaning, which
is "*eigen*," "own." Thus, the verb *sich ereignen* says: "to
bring into one's own," or "to come into one's own." Holding
this together with the surface meaning of "to come to pass," we
arrive at the phrase "to transpire by coming into its own."
For simplicity's sake, however, in what follows, we shall usually
translate *Ereignis* with "bringing-into-ownness."

The flashing of Da-sein in which Da-sein turns into its own
truth and thereby owns the danger as danger, i.e., discloses it
as such, is bringing-into-ownness. Bringing-into-ownness is
the sudden transpiring of truth, a transpiring in which Da-sein
clears itself and thereby comes into its own.

> The turning of the danger transpires by coming
> into its own suddenly. In this turning, the
> clearing [*Lichtung*] belonging to the prevailing
> [*Wesen*] of being suddenly clears itself. This
> sudden self-clearing is the lightning-flash. It
> brings itself into its own brightness, which it
> itself both brings along and brings in. When, in
> the turning of the danger, the truth of being
> flashes, the prevailing of being clears itself.
> Then the truth of the prevailing of being turns
> and enters in.32

Bringing-into-ownness is thus the name that Heidegger uses for
the transpiring of primordial relatedness on its own terms, the
clearing of the mystery at the heart of that relatedness, the
coming into its own of the mystery as mystery.

This last point is confirmed by several of Heidegger's
discussions of bringing-into-ownness. "Der Satz der Identität"
concludes with a discussion of bringing-into-ownness as the
transpiring of the *belonging* together of man and being. In the
terms of this essay, bringing-into-ownness is thus the coming
into its own of the primordial relatedness which undergirds any

distinction of man and being.[33] In another place, Heidegger
discusses bringing-into-ownness as the ultimate context of
derivation and explanation which itself cannot be derived or in
any way explained, but which must simply be received in the
mystery of its own transpiring.

> There is nothing else from which bringing-into-
> ownness itself could be derived, even less in
> whose terms it could be explained. Bringing-
> into-ownness is not the outcome (result) of
> something else, but the giving yield whose
> giving reach alone is what gives us such possi-
> bilities as a "there is given" [es gibt], a
> "there is given" of which even being itself
> stands in need so as to come into its own as
> coming-to-presence.[34]

If bringing-into-ownness is thus the name that Heidegger
uses for the coming-into-its-own of the mystery of Da-sein as
such, the mystery which in its essential withholding from presence threatens itself with oblivion in the triumph of gathering-
into-orderability, then with bringing-into-ownness we come again
to the simple ultimate that cannot be characterized except as
itself by itself. In other words, just as we concluded at the
beginning of this chapter that transcendence is ultimately
irreducible mystery, now we similarly conclude that bringing-
into-ownness is the coming-into-its-own of the mystery of world.
This coming-into-its-own is itself the most mysterious, and
accordingly, the final word that can be said of it is this:
"das Er-Eignis ereignet," "the transpiring that brings into its
own transpires by bringing into its own."[35]

Even though we seem to have come full circle back to the
beginning of this chapter, this does not mean that we have
simply returned to the same point from which we began. We began
with the irreducible mystery of Da-sein, and now we have returned
to that mystery, but with the addition of the name bringing-into-
ownness. In bringing-into-ownness, mystery transpires to "accomplish" (non-volitionally) what we could not have done, namely it
characterizes itself, although not in categorial or conceptual
fashion. In the transpiring of bringing-into-ownness, primordial
mystery characterizes itself as coming-into-ownness, as enownment,[36] as the gathering of everything into ownness, and the
self-clearing of this gathering as gathering-into-ownness. In

this characterization, two features are discernable: First,
ownness itself, and second, the clearing and illuminating of
this ownness as such.

With regard to the first feature, bringing-into-ownness
transpires to bring everything into its own, into ownness, and
this means to bring all things into the singular, all-appro-
priating context of their coming-to-presence. In bringing-into-
ownness, the thing is thus owned by world and vice-versa. In
bringing-into-ownness, world, thing and human being are all
brought into their essential nearness, into their mutual owning
or belonging. In bringing-into-ownness, thing owns world and
human being as its own; world owns thing and human being as its
own, and human being owns world and thing as its own. All are
brought together into the ownness of their mutual owning. Although this language may seem forced, we have already seen an
example of such enownment when we discovered the jug's being to
be the fourfold of world, which we can now indicate as the jug's
owning of world, and the world's owning of jug in bringing-into-
ownness. Similarily, the ownness of human being and world, or
human being and thing, could also be used as exemplifying
bringing-into-ownness.

With regard to the second feature, the illuminating, the
clearing, of ownness, bringing-into-ownness transpires as the
infusion of mystery into the totality of all that is. Bringing-
into-ownness thereby illuminates itself as mystery, as the
mystery of ownness which pervades and appropriates all that is.
It is in this sense that Heidegger says, *"Ereignis ist eignende
Eräugnis,"* "Bringing-into-ownness is enowning that brings to
sight."[37] It is the bringing into ownness which brings to sight.
This means that in the enowning of bringing-into-ownness, all
that is is "caught sight of," all humans are "caught sight of,"
and are thereby themselves brought into the sphere of enowning
illumination.

This "being caught sight of" does not mean that beings, and
we humans among them, are perceived in some primordial or
grounding consciousness. Instead, it means that the flashing
of world-openness as enowning, as the gathering into ownness
and the illumination of all in this ownness, is itself the gift
of sight, that which brings us and beings into the *nearness*

which is the basis of the appropriation accomplished in our
seeing (or hearing, etc.) anything at all. We see, because we
have already been owned by, and thus brought into the nearness
of, the luminous realm of bringing-into-ownness, the realm of
primordial sighting. Sight thus does not stem from man, but
instead man sees because in bringing-into-ownness, all that is,
including humans, are "sighted" and thereby brought into the
ownness of the sphere of sight.[38] In thus being "sighted,"
human being is drawn into the illumination of Da-sein and is
thereby *enabled* to encounter mystery as such.

We may now conclude this discussion of bringing-into-
ownness by returning to the issue of the fourfold of meaning.
We had questioned Heidegger's account of the fourfold on the
basis of the challenge to Da-sein posed by its own destined
oblivion in the triumph of gathering-into-orderability. Now we
see that we do not need to choose between the alternative characterizations of Da-sein as the fourfold and as gathering-into-
orderability. Instead, we now see that Da-sein, even though it
prevails for the most part in its own oblivion, nevertheless
also counterprevails in strife against oblivion and gives itself, however rarely, as bringing-into-ownness, as the happening
of its own truth. And it is as bringing-into-ownness that the
fourfold prevails.

Bringing-into-ownness enowns, shows ownness to *pervade* the
discreteness of the particular, and also illuminates the mystery
of ownness as such. But how does ownness occur most pervasively
in bringing-into-ownness? As the fourfold of meaning, the fourfold of world. In terms of bringing-into-ownness, we can now
understand the *oneness* of the fourfold. Earth and sky, the Holy
and death, are all enowned, allowed to prevail in their mutual
belonging in bringing-into-ownness. When Da-sein flashes as
bringing-into-ownness, infusing mystery into the totality of
all that is, then the four domains of meaning are brought close
in the thing, and in human perceiving of the thing. They prevail as the primordial dimensions of ownness, the articulation
of the singularity of transcendent meaning.

In bringing-into-ownness, therefore, man is brought into
his being owned and his owning of divinity. Man is brought
before the Holy, and the Holy is brought before man. As enowned

in bringing-into-ownness, man reaches up into the Holy, experiences the distance of divinity in the nearness of the Holy,
and thus experiences himself as measured by this divine distance-
in-nearness. Only because earth and sky, divinities and mortal
man are brought into the mystery of ownness, there to confront
each other as enowned and thus as essentially belonging to the
oneness of enownment itself, is there given for man the experience of divinity, and thus the encounter with God or the gods.
As Heidegger has said:

> Whether the god lives or remains dead is not decided
> by the religiosity of man and even less by the
> theological aspirations of philosophy and natural
> science. Whether or not God is God transpires by
> bringing into its own from out of and within the
> constellation of being.

And then he asks:

> Will we arrive within the prevailing of the nearness
> that brings near the world which things in the thing?
> Will we dwell as those at home in nearness, so that
> we will belong primally within the fourfold of sky
> and earth, mortals and divinities?[39]

Will we? It is not for us to say. For bringing-into-ownness
and its infusion of mystery, its illumination of ownness,
essentially surpasses and transcends our ability to forecast
and to compute, much less our ability to control.

CHAPTER V

TOWARD A "POST-THEISTIC" THEOLOGY

In the previous chapter, we discovered that the danger threatening Da-sein is not a danger to which Da-sein completely and utterly succumbs. In the midst of the triumph of gathering-into-orderability (oblivion), Da-sein may yet flash as itself, and in so flashing disclose itself as the final context of coming-to-presence, a context which characterizes itself as "ownness," as the bringing-into-ownness of all that comes forth as anything at all in particular. In the disclosure of Da-sein as bringing-into-ownness, the danger is overcome and Da-sein is saved.

To speak of bringing-into-ownness is to speak of the funda-mental and pervasive "trait" in which all beings, we humans included, may be manifest. This trait is not the trait which rules in gathering-into-orderability, i.e., simple and discrete particularity (which we have termed "incidentality"), but rather the trait of "ownness" which collects all into mutuality. It is the "ownness" of all beings in the sense of the world-exten-sive expanse of their essential inter-involvement and hence the world-extensiveness of their very being. To see something in the flash of bringing-into-ownness is to see it as a particular configuration of world, and hence to see its particularity not as discrete but rather as a "nodal intersection" of the world's primary meaning-domains. It is to see the world-domains of meaning brought close and brought into non-particular oneness in the full extent of the thing's coming-to-presence. It is to see the being of the thing as this very nodal gathering of world.

Bringing-into-ownness thus overcomes the incidentality of merely particular beings as these are revealed under the sway of gathering-into-orderability. In bringing-into-ownness, beings are revealed as enowned in the fourfold of meaning. In bring-ing-into-ownness, beings are *how* they are precisely insofar as earth and sky, the Holy and death are brought close as the

interpenetrating "aspects" of the thing's coming-to-presence.
A being comes-to-presence as already owning, and being owned
by, the self-enclosing impenetrability of earth, the open inviting expansiveness of sky, the insurmountable and noncircumventible claim of the Holy, and the transcience, the non-
recoverability, of death.

Another way of elucidating this trait of ownness is to
speak of it in terms of part and whole. The customary conceptual
distinction of part and whole pre-grasps the part atomistically
and the whole as the simple sum of the parts. However, bringing-
into-ownness reveals the "relation" of part and whole to be
quite different than the sum of atomistic individuals. The
whole, conceived as a mere sum, is incidental to the being of
the atomistic individual. But bringing-into-ownness overcomes
such incidentality by disclosing the whole as prevailing in and
as essential to the parts. The "wholeness" of things is not
incidental, but instead is quite fundamental to the presencing
of things. In bringing-into-ownness, the whole is restored to
its primacy over the merely particular. The whole thus gathers
the particulars into their fundamental commonality, a commonality
which overcomes the alienation of distance when distance is
gauged and experienced from within the standpoint of the internal
identity of the merely particular.

To pursue this line of thought, one can also speak of
bringing-into-ownness in terms of the distinction of identity
and difference. Customarily, identity and difference are simply
opposing relations. As we have suggested earlier, the simple
opposition of identity and difference characterizes the merely
actual insofar as actuality involves coming to a stand based
upon the self-coincidence of internal identity. And this is to
say that mere actuality results from a pervasive "thrust" of
being into internal self-same identity and external difference.
The actual is thus relatively self-sufficient and self-contained
by virtue of its external difference from what is not itself.
Hence, the coming-into-appearance of the merely actual rests
upon the pervasive separation of identity from difference as
ontological traits, a separation which characterizes gathering-
into-orderability.

In the merely actual, identity refers to the self-same or
self-coincident thing, A = A. On the other hand, difference is
a totally other relation than identity. An actual thing is
different from other actual things, but is not identical to
those other things. And correlatively, an actual thing is
identical to itself but is not different from itself.

Because actuality involves the sepration of identity from
difference, the hallmark of actuality is separate or independent
existence. To be actual, i.e., self-identical, is to be self-
standing and hence to be essentially separated from that which
lies beyond the parameters of internal self-coincidence. The
actual thing is separated out into its standing, independent
identity, identity is merely opposed to difference, part is
separated from whole.

However, in bringing-into-ownness, identity and difference
no longer occur as merely opposing relations. Instead, the
differences which attend particularity do not overcome the
singular wholeness which pervades and enowns those differences
into an underlying mutuality. Identity is thus not concentrated
into the individual and particular thing, but is allowed to rule
as the pervasive sameness gathing all of world-openness into the
commonality of something's coming-into-presence. Identity thus
infuses difference and difference infuses identity. They are
no longer opposed, but are disclosed in bringing-into-ownness
to belong essentially to each other.

In connection with this discussion of identity and difference, we may digress a bit and speak once again of the customary
interpretation of divine transcendence as the perfection of
being, this time keeping in mind our preceding discussion of the
essence of actuality. As we said, this essence lies in the
separation of identity and difference into merely opposing relations. Now, if divine transcendence is interpreted in terms of
the supposed primacy of the actual, such transcendence will be
understood as the perfection of the essential traits of actuality.
The two traits we have mentioned are internal self-coincidence
(identity), on the one hand, and external difference, on the
other. The perfection of the first trait, internal identity,
would be complete self-sufficiency, the absolute sufficiency of
something for its own coming-to-presence. Such absolute

self-sufficiency would involve an internal identity of knower
and known, or to put it more aptly, of presence and that which
receives presence. The perfection of the second trait, external
difference, would be essential separation. In the perfection
of external difference, no real or essential relations to what
is different can in fact take place. The perfect self-sufficiency of its internal identity is in principle unaffected and
undisturbed by whatever is differentiated from that identity.
The perfection of each of these traits of actuality is suggested
in classical Thomistic theism. However, if the primacy of the
actual is not presupposed, then the meaning of divine transcendence may be understood differently than as the perfection of
identity and difference in internal self-sufficiency and essential
separation from the other, respectively.

As we may now see, bringing-into-ownness discloses identity
and difference as mutually infusing, pervasive traits, rather
than as merely opposing relations. Accordingly, it may serve
as the basis for interpreting divine transcendence in a way that
does not presuppose the primacy of the actual and thus that does
not culminate in an interpretation of divine transcendence rooted
in the notions of absolute internal self-sufficiency and essential
separation from the other.

At this point we may now take up once again the question of
the meaning of transcendence as such. When we last interrupted
our direct discussion of this question, we had established that
the meaning of transcendence as such can be raised only as the
question of the way in which humans experience themselves as
measured in the emergent claim of divinity. In other words,
transcendence occurs as the divine measure of that which is
essential to human being. Based on this, we now suggest that
the divine names the emergent "standard" against which we come
to understand human wholeness. The divine is the emergent source
or fount of human well-being, that in relation to which we first
understand and receive genuine human health. In another language,
this is to say that the divine is the source of salvation.

Transcendence as such can accordingly be interpreted only
as the way in which Da-sein may prevail so as to grant the
occurrence of human well-being, or at least the understanding of
what this would essentially entail. Thus, transcendence can be

sought only insofar as Da-sein brings human being into wholeness, and thereby discloses the measure of human well-being. But as we have seen, such bringing-into-wholeness is not universally characteristic of Da-sein's manner of prevailing. Instead, humans are brought into wholeness only insofar as Da-sein counterprevails against its own destined oblivion and flashes as such in bringing-into-ownness. Only in such flashing is human being granted the singular wholeness of its essential home. Given this proviso, we can now ask: Insofar as bringing-into-ownness flashes in the midst of Da-sein's oblivion, how is transcendence as such to be encountered in the claim of divinity?

Beyond the Absence of Divinity: Coming Home to the Pure Unknown

One could attempt to characterize the way in which divinity now claims human being and still remain wedded to the thinking, predominant under the rule of gathering-into-orderability, which accords primacy to particular, discrete things (i.e., to the *actual*). In this event, one is inevitably forced to say that divinity now encounters human being only in the limiting mode of *absence*. To be sure, much has been said of late concerning "the absence of divinity in our time." But does the term "absence" genuinely speak the way in which the Holy is now open as grant, as allowance, and as claim in bringing-into-ownness? Or does it rather speak from the darkening, the closing of world which reigns in the triumph of bringing-into-orderability (oblivion)?

In our earlier discussion of Da-sein, we said that the *path* to the encounter with Da-sein as such is the Nothing (Chapter III, pp. 93ff, especially note 72, pp. 161-162. At that time, we also stated that this term, "the Nothing," is not intended as a final characterization of the primordial realm of meaning, but is intended instead as a preliminary designation of the "entrance" to this realm which a thoughtful pursuit must pass through.

We may now expand this point in connection with the purported "absence" of divinity which we now encounter. If one's characterization of the primordial realm of meaning were exhausted in the term "Nothing," then given the current absence of determinate epiphanies of divinity, one would perforce conclude that ours is

indeed the age in which the divine is absent. However, if
"Nothing" is but a preliminary characterization pertaining to the
entree now given for a thoughtful approach to the primordial
realm, then talk of the absence of the divine may also be preliminary (although not on that account incorrect, at least as
far as it goes).

The divine is indeed absent if by that is meant that no
actual manifestation of divinity is now experienced to occur,
that no determinate epiphany occurs. As we have seen, all determinate presentment is now for the most part entrapped under the
rule of gathering-into-orderability. Things are now seen *only
in their particularities*, only in the manner of the incidental
which is the sole allowance of coming-into-presence that gathering-into-orderability sustains. Nothing that we have said concerning bringing-into-ownness undercuts this phenomenological
claim. Thus, no determinate manifestations of divinity are now
to be encountered, as long as gathering-into-orderability holds
undisputed sway. We thus live in the absence of divinity, as
long as and to the extent that our ek-sistence is opened only
onto the particularities, the incidentality, of beings.

However, this is not to say that there is no going beyond
such absence of divinity. For in addition to the now-prevailing
rule of gathering-into-orderability which elevates particularity
to an exclusive position, there may also transpire the flashing
of bringing-into-ownness. If we are to go beyond the absence of
divinity, then this can only be if and how this going-beyond is
granted in such flashing.

To say how it is that absence of divinity is transcended,
we must pay heed to what has already been said concerning bringing-into-ownness. Bringing-into-ownness overcomes the rule of
incidentality in that it is the gathering of the fourfold domain
of meaning into the particular thing. It overcomes the separation of identity from difference, and thus overcomes discreteness
as the basic trait of beings. Bringing-into-ownness gathers
world (difference) into the thing (identity). In this gathering,
the thing is disclosed to be more than its determinate particularity (i.e., its supposedly internal identity). It is instead
seen to be the nodal intersection in which the world's primary
meaning-domains are gathered into oneness. Thus, the flashing

of bringing-into-ownness carries beyond particularity as such
into the mutual owning of earth, sky, the Holy, and death, an
owning which occurs in the identity-in-difference of the thing's
presencing.

In addition to this, we have also noted that the Holy is
the meaning-domain which yields direct encounter with the transcendence of meaning as such. As the Holy opens up in the
flashing of bringing-into-ownness, one is encountered by the
noncircumventibility of the claim of meaning. How is one claimed
in this opening of the Holy? One is claimed for the mystery of
ownness itself. One is brought into the disclosedness of ownness,
and is given ownness as one's essential preserve. One thus ek-
sists not merely to preserve the truth (i.e., the manifestness)
of *particular* beings. More fundamental than this, one is granted
as one's ek-sistent dwelling the truth, the unique disclosedness,
of primordial ownness itself in its unique singularity. This
ownness, this wholeness, which prevails before all things and
which pervades all things as inherent in their coming forth
claims ek-sistent human being for its own in the opening up of
the Holy.

May we, then, speak of divinity and not merely of the absence of divinity? We may, if by divinity we do not mean an
occurrence of the actual, if we do not mean a manifestation which
holds itself in internal identity separated out from what is
other. Insofar as bringing-into-ownness flashes, we live not
merely in the absence of the divine, but in addition may be
taken beyond such absence into the non-actual divine ownness
which pervades all actual particularity.

Our claim is that the divine may yet prevail, although not
in accordance with the incidentality, the concentration into
internal identity, that now characterizes particular things in
their actuality. How then does the divine yet prevail? At this
point we need to recall our basic phenomenological claim regarding Da-sein, namely, that Da-sein as such does not culminate in
any trans-emergent structure of presence, but rather extends
essentially into irreducible mystery. In mystery, Da-sein
discloses itself as surpassing any possible cognition, any
possible grasping of something in a concept, and hence any
possible explanation in terms of the interconnections permissible

in some conceptual scheme. Thus, Da-sein as such is the essential Unknown. It is the primordial oneness which cannot be
grasped but can yet be encountered precisely as ungraspable.

In bringing-into-ownness, Da-sein is encountered as "unify-
ing," as that which brings *close*, not in the usual sense of
measurable distance along some calculable dimension, but in the
sense of nearness to one's being, the nearness which belongs to
and thus enhances, rather than diminishing or destroying, one's
being. Bringing-close in this sense is thus encountered as the
enhancement of one's own, and the withering away of what is
essentially alien and thus a diminishing of the sphere of one's
own. In bringing-into-ownness, one encounters the world itself
as brought into one's own, and one encounters oneself as delivered over to the owning of world. One encounters the essential
Unknown as the sphere of one's own, as the fount of one's
essential being. Thus, bringing-into-ownness is divine in that
from it flows essential well-being, the measure of human health.

In the opening up of the Holy, one encounters the claim of
the essential Unknown. One encounters oneself in this claim to
be insurmountably owned by the essential Unknown. In what sense
is one "owned" by the essential Unknown? Not in the sense of
property. One is not enslaved in being thus owned. One is not
the chattel of the essential Unknown. Instead, one is owned by
being brought into one's own. Thus, one is not owned in the
sense of "possessed," but is called forth into the sphere that
is already one's own, and thus one is set free. One thereby
attains to freedom in the deepest sense of the term. One is set
free by the grant of reconciliation, the grant which overcomes
the split between *what* one is in particular, and *how* one is
essentially in the sphere of one's own. In being claimed for
the essential Unknown, one is brought forth out of bondage to
one's particularity and is set free into one's essential freedom,
the freedom of ek-sistent Da-sein which breaks through the
restricting parameters of determinacy itself.

The word which best names the situation of being set free
by being brought into one's own is "home." In the claim of the
Holy, therefore, one encounters the essential Unknown as *home*.
This is the grace of the divine. One is enowned and thereby
brought home into essential mystery. Mystery, the Unknown, is

no longer experienced as the place of evil and of danger, against
which we pit, in Sisyphean effort, our meager cognitive and
calculative powers. Instead, it is itself experienced as home,
as the preserve to which our ek-sistence essentially belongs.
It is experienced in homecoming as the true "identity" of one's
being, as the "wholeness" or "salvation" to which we are essentially directed.

This, then, is how the divine now transpires in the rare
flashing of Da-sein as bringing-into-ownness. At least, this
is what we can say if we follow the hints which Heidegger's
thinking affords. The divine transpires not as incidental actuality but as the pervasive *at-homeness* of essential mystery, the
essential Unknown. The divine is the self-granting of mystery
as home. It is the noncircumventible claim which drafts human
ek-sistence into its home in mystery. It is the claim which
brings humans home to the freedom which lies beyond any internal
"freedom" of the actual, and thus beyond actual self-assertive
volition itself. In other words, the divine *is* the "revelation,"
the disclosure of mystery itself as one's free and essential
dwelling-place, a disclosure which overcomes the otherwise
hegemonistic rule of gathering-into-orderability.

The Meaning of Transcendence as Such

Little more need be said concerning the meaning of transcendence as such. Transcendence means surpassing fixed limit,
boundary, determination. In bringing-into-ownness, transcendence
is disclosed as such. It is revealed not as separate actuality,
a self-sufficient or self-coincident being, but instead as the
wholeness pervading particularity, a wholeness which constitutes
the essential preserve of human ek-sistence. It is revealed as
the indeterminate, non-actual home of human being.

In the opening of the Holy in bringing-into-ownness, man
receives his essential measure. Man is measured as the one who
is owned by the essential Unknown, and thus as the one who finds
himself and his genuine well-being only in the at-homeness of the
essential Unknown. The grant of the essential Unknown as the
human home claims man in the Holy. This claim is the transpiring of divinity. The meaning of transcendence is thus: Essential mystery bringing human ek-sistence home to itself and

to its non-actual yet salvific identity-in-difference or ownness.

The Need for a "Post-Theistic" Theology

In the just-mentioned meaning of transcendence as such, it
is to be noted that this meaning is a *way* that Da-sein as primordial relatedness itself prevails. Transcendence is neither
an "attribute" of human being per se nor an actuality separate
from human being. Instead, it is the way that primordial relatedness gathers both human ek-sistence and all present actualities
into the all-inclusive oneness of being-at-home.

An implication of this understanding of transcendence is
that the traditional attempts to bring the Unknown into self-
identity and hence into actual, determinate presentment are
found to be unsatisfactory. Transcendence does not attain to
self-identical presence (actuality). Instead, transcendence
remains withdrawal-from-presence. Thus, insofar as traditional
theism is wedded to the affirmation of a self-identical, self-
actualizing deity, even one whose self-actualizing identity is
in everlasting process, such theology runs counter to the
thinking presented here. In place of such theology, a "post-
theistic" theology is needed, one which is not wedded to the
affirmation of a deity which comes into its own identity and
thus essentially comes-to-presence (even if never within human
experience).

But in speaking of "post-theistic" theology, we do not
thereby necessarily mean an anti-Christian theology. Indeed, one
could suggest that the theology proposed here runs parallel to a
central trajectory of Christian thinking concerning the divine,
namely its *incarnationalism*. The theology proposed here is in a
sense an incarnational one in that the meaning of transcendence
as such is not to be found in an actuality essentially separate
from human being, but is rather to be found in the way that human
ek-sistence is owned by its own Da-sein. Transcendence is thus
incarnate, i.e., is to be found in and as human ek-sistence, but
is not thereby reduced to an ontic component of world (e.g.,
human subjectivity as opposed to non-subjective "reality").
Transcendence is incarnate in human ek-sistence whenever in the
grace of the flashing of bringing-into-ownness, one is claimed

for the preservation of the at-homeness of essential mystery.
But this "incarnation" is not restricted to any single individual or period of history. This last point may suggest a "post-
Christian" as well as a post-theistic theology. But this is
not a claim that we wish now to advance. Suffice it to say
that whenever and for whomever bringing-into-ownness flashes
is not something subject to human influence, prediction or
control. Its occurrence is the essence of grace. And thus,
we can ourselves entertain no restriction on this flashing of
grace. We can only receive its grant when we are claimed by it.
Of course, all of this leaves unanswered whether or not an
"original incarnation" of bringing-into-ownness can be recognized
historically and whether or not such an "original" would assume
any special or authoritative position relative to temporally
subsequent "incarnations." But again these are questions which
lie outside of the scope of the present work.

The Question of God

By way of conclusion, we here offer a few remarks concerning the question of God. As we have indicated above, if the
term "God" names *a* being which comes-to-presence in some kind
of self-identity and thus is actual, a differentiable even if
supreme reality, then the theology proposed here allows no room
for the name "God." The being of God cannot be understood in
terms of the being of beings, i.e., coming-to-presence. Therefore, one cannot even speak of the being of God.

However, if we do not restrict the term "God" to the metaphysics of coming-to-presence, then the term "God" may be
retained. But how is this name to be understood, if "God" does
not name *a* being? It should be obvious by now that it is in-
appropriate here simply to identify God with being itself. Being
itself is coming-to-presence, and there is no religious reason,
or any else for that matter, for saying that "God" is merely a
synonym for "being."

These, however, are not the only alternatives. As we have
seen, Da-sein prevails as an essential strife or conflict. On
the one hand, Da-sein prevails as the triumph of gathering-into-
orderability and hence as the threat, the danger, of its own
oblivion. However, Da-sein also counterprevails against its

own oblivion. It counterprevails in the flashing of bringing-
into-ownness, in which the danger of oblivion inherent in the
triumph of gathering-into-orderability is encountered *as such*.

In light of this, we now wish to propose that the name
"God" cannot be used as a strict synonym for Da-sein as such,
but instead names Da-sein *in its counterprevailing*, in its
flashing as bringing-into-ownness. "God" names the grace of
bringing-into-ownness, the grace which transpires when human
ek-sistence is brought home into its own in essential mystery.

"God" thus does not name a being which attains to self-
identity and thereby comes-to-presence, but instead names the
"saving" of Da-sein in its counterprevailing against its own
self-granted destiny. Da-sein is divine insofar as it refuses
fully to nihilate itself in the triumph of its destiny (gathering-into-orderability). "God" accordingly names the *way* in
which Da-sein saves itself, and thereby the way in which Da-sein
gives itself as the mystery of ownness for ek-sistent preservation. When one is called home for such preservation, when one
experiences the wholeness which prevails throughout all particularity and experiences oneself as belonging to and preserving
in ek-sistent reception such wholeness within particularity,
such identity-in-difference, than one has encountered God, the
divine.

Can we then speak of the *being* of God, or of the *reality*
of God? Not without introducing somewhat misleading and con-
fusing language. The being of anything is *how* it comes to
presence, how it is *as* something or other. But "ownness" itself
does not come to presence. It is rather the way in which, precisely as withdrawal-from-presence, Da-sein gathers all that
does come to presence into a prevailing context of enowning
mutuality. Thus, there is no being, no coming-to-presence, of
the grace of ownness itself. And this in turn means that the
phrase "the being of God" is misleading at best. It is also
misleading to speak of the "reality" of God, insofar as the term
"reality" entails a being that attains to some manner of self-
identity and hence to some determinate coming-to-presence (being).

Instead of speaking of the "being" of God, or the "reality"
of God, one would do better to speak of the "grace" of God,
the "way" of the divine, the "how" of the divine prevailing.

In this way, one stays closer to the experience of the divine
claim itself, a claim which occurs *as claim* and not as determinate presence. What is religiously significant is not that
God be understood as an actual reality. Instead, religious
significance derives from the encounter with the "saving" that
is experienced when one is "brought home" into the heart of the
divine Unknown.

CHAPTER I

NOTES

[1]"The concept of transcendence stems from the notion of a boundary to what is given and available. Beyond this boundary there is assumed to be a heterogeneous, unconditioned, non-objectifiable reality....Accordingly, the concept of transcendence designates the absolute difference between the conditioned (world) and its ontological foundation, as well as this foundation itself insofar as it evades every theoretical inquiry and practical availability." *Die Religion in Geschichte und Gegenwart*, 3rd ed., s.v. "Transcendenz und Immanenz," by H. Blumenberg (my translation).

[2]This account of the meaning of "transcendence" is in part gleaned from the following sources: Lewis and Short, *A Latin Dictionary*, 1879, s.v. "*scandō*"; A. Ernout and A. Meillet, *Dictionnaire Etymologique de la Langue Latine*, 4th ed., s.v. "*scandō*"; *The American Heritage Dictionary of the English Language*, 1969, 1970, s.v. the Indo-European root "*skand*"; *The Oxford English Dictionary*, 1961 ed., s.v. "transcend" "transcendence."

[3]These attempts were in large measure initiated by Dietrich Bonhoeffer's suggestive reflections in his posthumously published *Letters and Papers from Prison* (New York: Macmillan Co., 1971). A good example of this is found in the following passage: "I should like to speak of God not on the boundaries but at the center, not in weakness but in strength; and therefore not in death and guilt but in man's life and goodness....The transcendence of epistemological theory has nothing to do with the transcendence of God. *God is beyond in the midst of life.*" (p. 282, emphasis mine) In addition to Bonhoeffer, Paul Tillich's work was also quite seminal in initiating the search for the presence of transcendence within the secularity of modern culture. See especially his essay "Religion and Secular Culture," *The Protestant Era*, abridged ed. (Chicago: University of Chicago Press, 1957), pp. 55-65, in which he attempts "to show that in the depth of every autonomous culture an ultimate concern, something unconditional and holy, is implied" (p. 58). More recently, theologians such as Schubert Ogden, Langdon Gilkey, John Cobb and others have attempted to pursue this search.

[4]An exception to this understanding of transcendence as perfectly and *immediately* self-sufficient is provided by Hegelian thought. In Hegel one finds a recognition of the inexpugnable need for externality inherent in the life of Absolute Spirit. The self-contemplation of Absolute Spirit is thus not immediate, but instead is mediated through the diremption into externality that characterizes the historical world of human experience. Nevertheless, Absolute Spirit overcomes externality through *dialectical* self-completion, mediated self-completion which overcomes the externality of historical life through the

147

establishment of ever more encompassing levels of identity
(immediate identity *through* difference). Accordingly, even
Hegelian thought understands transcendence in terms of perfect,
albeit mediated, self-completion.

[5]"Owning" will play a central role in our interpretation
of transcendence. See below, Chapters IV and V.

CHAPTER II

NOTES

[1] Ludwig Wittgenstein, *Tractatus Logico-Philosophicus* (London: Routledge and Kegan Paul, 1922). Hereafter, all references to this text will be given in parentheses within the body of our text, by citing the number of the relevant proposition.

[2] See, for example, Wittgenstein's *Philosophical Investigations* (New York: The Macmillan Co., 1953), paragraphs 23, 41, 43 (pp. 11-12, 20-21).

[3] Hans Georg Gadamer, *Wahrheit und Methode*, 3rd ed. (Tübingen: J. C. B. Mohr, 1972), p. 142 (E.T.: *Truth and Method* [New York: The Seabury Press, 1975], p. 134).

[4] *Wahrheit und Methode*, pp. 383-395 (E.T., pp. 366-378).

[5] *Wahrheit und Methode*, p. 391 (E.T., pp. 374-375). Translation slightly altered.

[6] Plato *Cratylus* 384c-d (*The Collected Dialogues of Plato*, ed. Edith Hamilton and Huntington Cairns, Bollingen Series LXXI [New York: Pantheon Books, 1961], p. 422).

[7] Ibid., 386d-e (E.T., pp. 424-425). See also 439e-440d (pp. 473-474).

[8] Ibid., 388a-b (E.T., p. 426). It should be noted here that the Greek word for "name," *onoma*, is also the Greek word for "word."

[9] Ibid., 390d-e (E.T., p. 429).

[10] Ibid., 431a-d (E.T., p. 465).

[11] Ibid., 435d-e (E.T., pp. 469-470).

[12] Ibid., 421d-422d (E.T., pp. 456-457).

[13] Ibid., 424b-c (E.T., p. 459).

[14] Ibid., 424c-425b (E.T., pp. 459-460).

[15] Ibid., 432b-e (E.T., pp. 466-467).

[16] Ibid., 435a-d (E.T., p. 469).

[17] Ibid., 438-439b (E.T., pp. 471-473).

[18] Ibid., 439b (E.T., p. 473).

[19] Plato *Seventh Letter* 343a (*The Collected Dialogues of Plato*, ed. Hamilton and Cairns, p. 1590).

150   The Meaning of Transcendence

[20]Gadamer, *Wahrheit und Methode*, p. 387 (cf. E.T., p. 370).
My translation.

[21]Alfred North Whitehead, *Process and Reality* (New York:
the Macmillan Co., 1929), p. 31. See also the discussion of
"the principle of process," pp. 34-35.

[22]Ibid., p. 46.

[23]Ibid., p. 521f.

[24]Ibid., p. 523.

[25]*Wahrheit und Methode*, pp. 392-395 (E.T., 375-378).

[26]*Wahrheit und Methode*, p. 389 (cf., E.T., p. 372). My
translation.

[27]"Language itself has a speculative character...as the
accomplishment of meaning, as the occurrence of speech, of
communication, of understanding. The speculative is such an
accomplishment, in that the finite possibilities of words are
disposed in their intended meaning, as in directedness toward
the infinite....To say what one means, to make oneself understood...is to hold what is said together with an infinity of
what is unsaid in the unity of a meaning and to let it be
understood as such." *Wahrheit und Methode*, pp. 444-445 (cf.,
E.T., p. 426). My translation.

[28]"Anyone who has experienced a lawsuit--even if only as a
witness--knows what it is to make a statement and how little it
is a statement of what one means. In a statement the horizon
of meaning of what must actually be said is concealed with
methodical exactness. What remains is the "pure" sense of
statements. That is what goes on record. But as meaning thus
reduced to what is stated it is always distorted meaning."
Wahrheit und Methode, p. 444 (E.T., p. 426). Translation
slightly altered.

[29]*Wahrheit und Methode*, p. 441 (E.T., p. 423). Translation
slightly altered.

[30]*Wahrheit und Methode*, pp. 131-132 (cf., E.T., pp. 122-
123). My translation.

[31]*Wahrheit und Methode*, p. 131 (cf., E.T., p. 122). My
translation.

[32]Martin Heidegger, *Sein und Zeit*, 12th ed. (Tübingen: Max
Niemeyer, 1972), pp. 153-160 (E.T.: *Being and Time*, trans.
John Macquarrie and Edward Robinson [New York: Harper & Row,
1962], pp. 194-203).

[33]Heidegger understands the existential-*hermeneutical* "as"
in terms of the circumspective fore-structure of understanding,
and he then takes the apophantic "as" to be a reduction or
"levelling-down" of the primordial circumspective "as" to the
level of mere presence-at-hand. See *Sein und Zeit*, pp. 156-158
(E.T., pp. 199-201).

[34]In an essay written much later than *Sein und Zeit*, entitled
"*Das Ding*" ("The Thing"), Heidegger himself gives an extended
illustration of his earlier distinction between the apophantic
and the hermeneutical "as." At the beginning of this essay,
Heidegger discusses the two primary philosophical interpretations
of pre-givenness relative to assertion, namely, realism and
idealism. He then selects an ordinary thing, a jug, and proceeds to describe its original appearance *as jug*, i.e., as a
world-extensive pattern of relatedness which itself is the being
of the jug's appearance as jug. Thus, this essay supports the
claim that the originary appearance of something is hermeneutical
and in this sense linguistic. "*Das Ding*," *Vorträge und Aufsätze*,
Teil II (Tübingen: Neske, 1967), pp. 37-55 (E.T.: "The Thing,"
Poetry, Language, Thought, trans. Albert Hofstadter [New York:
Harper & Row, 1971], pp. 165-186). For an extended discussion
of this essay see below, pp. 106-108.

[35]*Wahrheit und Methode*, p. 450 (E.T., p. 432). Translation
slightly altered.

[36]*Wahrheit und Methode*, p. 450 (cf., E.T., p. 432). My
translation.

[37]*Wahrheit und Methode*, p. 464 (E.T., p. 445). Translation
altered.

[38]It should be noted here that this characterization of
meaning is not yet an essential characterization. Here, meaning
is thought in relation to whatever shows itself, i.e., to beings.
But to inquire into the essence of meaning is not to interpret
meaning in terms of beings, but is rather to question after the
essence of meaning as such, i.e., to ask *how* it is that meaning
as such *prevails*.

[39]*Wahrheit und Methode*, p. 449 (E.T., p. 431). Translation
altered.

[40]For the present work, the understanding of world derives
primarily from Heidegger. The initial discussion of world in
Heidegger's work is to be found in the third chapter of *Sein
und Zeit*, entitled "Die Weltlichkeit der Welt," pp. 63-130,
especially section 18, pp. 83-88 (E.T., pp. 91-168, especially
pp. 114-123). The essay "Die Ursprung des Kunstwerkes"
(*Holzwege*, 5th ed. [Frankfurt am Main: Vittorio Klostermann,
1972], pp. 7-65; E.T.: *Poetry, Language, Thought*, pp. 15-87)
contains an important discussion of world. Here, world is
differentiated from all enumerable things and is seen to be the
pervasive, prevailing openness in which the essential directions
of destiny (i.e., foundational meanings) are laid down (Ibid.,
pp. 33-34; E.T., pp. 44-45). World is here contrasted with
earth, the latter naming the sheltering, self-secluding opaque-
ness which prevails, co-extensive with earth, as that out of
which beings come to a stand (Ibid., pp. 35-37; E.T., pp. 46-48).
At a later point in this essay, both world and earth as mutually
interrelated aspects are seen to belong to openness itself,
which now names the foundational emergence of the "conflict" or
mutual striving over against the other, in which both world and
earth originally emerge in their fundamental relatedness as and

how they are (Ibid., pp. 43-44; E.T., p. 55). In Heidegger's
later work, the world is seen as foundational openness itself,
which transpires as the fourfold unity that is comprised of the
"world-neighborhoods" in their mutual belonging to each other, a
belonging that occurs as a "mirror-play," and as the mutual
co-appropriating event [*Ereignis*] of world-openness (the "world-
ing of the world"). See *Vorträge und Aufsätze*, Teil II, pp. 23-
26, 50-55 (*Poetry, Language, Thought*, pp. 149-151, 178-182).
See also *Unterwegs zur Sprache* (Tübingen: Neske, 1959), pp. 208-
216 (E.T.: *On the Way to Language*, trans. Peter Hertz [New York:
Harper & Row, 1971], pp. 101-108). For a brief but helpful
discussion of the development of Heidegger's understanding of
world, see Werner Marx, *Heidegger and the Tradition* (Evanston:
Northwestern University Press, 1971), pp. 183-203.

[41]*Wahrheit und Methode*, p. 419 (cf., E.T., p. 401). My
translation.

[42]See e.g., *Wahrheit und Methode*, pp. 382, 415-432, 450
(E.T., pp. 365, 401-414, 432); also Hans Georg Gadamer, *Philosophical Hermeneutics*, trans. David E. Linge (Berkeley: University of California Press, 1976), pp. 3, 67, 77-78.

[43]It should be noted here that this thesis of Gadamer owes
much to Heidegger's later works on language, especially *Unterwegs zur Sprache*. Also, Wittgenstein in his later thought may
have approximated to this view of the ontological import of
language (and hence, meaning), specifically in his notion of
"form of life" [*lebensform*], which seems to function founda-
tionally in his thinking, i.e., is ontologically primary, and
yet is also determined by language: "'So you are saying that
human agreement decides what is true and what is false?'--True
and false are what human beings *say*, and it is in *language* that
they agree. This is no agreement in opinions [*Meinungen*] but
in the form of life." *Philosophical Investigations*, par. 241
(p. 88).

[44]However, recall our earlier discussion of the sameness
(albeit not strict identity) of the being of the word, and that
which comes to presence linguistically, pp. 38-41.

[45]Here, the term "medium" does not refer to something
through which something else passes, as in the case of the old
scientific notion of the "ether." Thus, language is not construed to be an external or partial mediation of the world.
Rather, language is the medium of world (and, *mutatis mutandis*
of the appearance of beings) in the same way that the lake is
the medium in which the castle comes to reflected appearance,
and along with it its context of understandability. The *being*
of the medium is one with the presentment itself, so that nothing
passes through something else. Gadamer's notion of "total
mediation" is relevant here. See *Wahrheit und Methode*, pp. 105-
115, 121 (E.T., pp. 99-108, 113).

[46]*Wahrheit und Methode*, p. 450 (cf., E.T., p. 432). My
translation.

[47]"What the world is is not different from the views in which it offers itself." *Wahrheit und Methode*, p. 423 (E.T., p. 406). Translation altered slightly.

[48]"It is language which really opens up the whole of our relatedness-in-the-world [*Weltverhaltens*]." *Wahrheit und Methode*, p. 425 (cf., E.T., p. 407). My translation. Also: "The experience of the world in language is 'absolute.' It transcends all the relativities of any positing of being [*Seinssetzung*], because it encompasses all being-in-itself, in whatever relations (relativities) it shows itself. The linguisticality of our experience of world is prior to everything that can be recognized and addressed as something that is [*als seiend*]." *Wahrheit und Methode*, p. 426 (E.T., p. 408). Translation altered.

[49]*Wahrheit und Methode*, p. 433 (E.T., p. 415). Translation altered.

[50]This is what Gadamer means when he says: "Nothing that is said has its truth simply in itself, but refers instead backward and forward to what is unsaid." *Philosophical Hermeneutics*, p. 67.

[51]"We start from the claim that the mode of being of the work of art is *presentation* [*Darstellung*], and then ask how the meaning of presentation is verified in what we call a picture." *Wahrheit und Methode*, p. 131. The English translation unfortunately renders *Darstellung* throughout this section as "representation," a rendering that fails to convey the sense of *original presentment*. See E.T., p. 122ff.

[52]*Wahrheit und Methode*, p. 133 (cf., E.T., p. 124). My translation; the published translation is here garbled.

[53]Heidegger's analysis of *Vorhandensein* as a derivative mode of thingly being is relevant here. See *Sein und Zeit*, sec. 15 (pp. 66-72).

[54]*Wahrheit und Methode*, p. 135 (E.T., pp. 125f).

[55]*Wahrheit und Methode*, p. 136 (E.T., p. 126). Translation slightly altered.

[56]Gadamer's claim that man's basic understanding of the world is the ongoing outcome of "effective-history" [*Wirkungsgeschichte*] is relevant here. In fact, the notion of *Wirkungsgeschichte* in Gadamer's thought replaces the notion of transcendental structure or self-identical essence as the foundation of the possibility of human understanding. See especially *Wahrheit und Methode*, pp. 284-290 (E.T., pp. 267-274).

[57]Gadamer's emphasis upon speculation raises the question of his relation to Heidegger's philosophy, especially in view of the fact that the latter is profoundly suspicious of the Hegelian claim that being emerges dialectically. See, for example, Heidegger's statement that the foundational "regioning" of world-openness [*die Gegnet*] should not be characterized as

"dialectical," in his *Gelassenheit* (Tübingen: Neske, 1959),
p. 68 (E.T.:   *Discourse on Thinking* [New York: Harper Torchbooks, 1966], p. 86).   In spite of this terminological difference, this writer agrees with Richard Palmer that there is no
fundamental discontinuity between Gadamer's understanding of the
speculative character of linguistic presentment and Heidegger's
concern that thought completely "release" itself to the nearing
and the distancing as which *die Gegnet* itself emerges.   See
Richard E. Palmer, *Hermeneutics* (Evanston: Northwestern University Press, 1969), pp. 215-217.   This judgment is possible
because Gadamer does not use the term "speculation" to mean the
coming-to-itself of a non-historical idea in the eventfulness
of history, but rather the unity of determinacy and indeterminacy
that always characterizes the event of linguistic presentment.
Similarly, *die Gegnet* for Heidegger is the unity of "nearing"
and "distancing" (See *Gelassenheit*, pp. 67-73).

[58]*Wahrheit und Methode*, p. 450 (E.T., p. 432).   Translation
altered.

[59]*Wahrheit und Methode*, p. 448 (E.T., p. 430).   Translation
altered.

[60]The German word usually translated "conditioned" is
bedingt.   This word literally means "be-thinged."   In the present context, an intersection or node of meaning-relations, i.e.,
a focused pattern of relations that allows a determinate self-
showing, is a "conditioned" possibility in the sense of "be-
thinged":   it is a definite way that the thing comes forth as a
"gathering" of world openness.

[61]*Wahrheit und Methode*, p. 444 (cf., E.T., p. 426).   My
translation.

[62]*Wahrheit und Methode*, p. 434 (E.T., p. 416).   Translation
altered slightly.

[63]*Wahrheit und Methode*, pp. 340, 344 (E.T., pp. 321, 325).

CHAPTER III

NOTES

[1]Anyone who wishes to trace the development in Heidegger's thinking is advised to consult the exhaustive work of William Richardson which does just that. William J. Richardson, S.J., *Heidegger: Through Phenomenology to Thought*, 2nd ed. (The Hague: Martinus Nijhoff, 1967)

[2]See our earlier discussion of "world," pp. 43-46.

[3]The overall claim of Heidegger concerning the primacy of understanding over explicit interpretation dovetails nicely with the general theory of meaning which we derived from Gadamer from the previous chapter.

[4]"Simply having something before one is to have it lie before one's pure gaze "*as a failure to understand it any longer.*" *Sein und Zeit*, p. 149 (cf., E.T., p. 190), my translation. Note also the following passage: "It has been shown how all sight is grounded in understanding. Thus...the primacy of pure intuition (*Anschauen*) is denied, which corresponds noetically with the primacy accorded by traditional ontology to the present-at-hand. 'Intuition' and 'thinking' are both already distant derivatives of understanding. Even the phenomenological 'intuition of essence' ('*Wesensschau*') is grounded in existential understanding." Ibid., p. 147 (cf., E.T., p. 187). My translation.

[5]"...when something within-the-world is encountered as such, it already has an involvement which is disclosed in our understanding of the world....The ready-to-hand is always already understood in terms of a totality of involvements." *Sein und Zeit*, p. 150 (E.T., pp. 190-191). Translation slightly altered.

[6]"This 'system of relations' as constituve of worldhood is so far from evaporating the being (*Sein*) of what is ready-to-hand within the world that such beings are only first uncovered in their 'substantial' 'in-itselfness' on the basis of the worldhood of the world." *Sein und Zeit*, p. 88 (cf., E.T., p. 122). My translation.

[7]"Understanding is the existential being of Dasein's own being-able-to-be [*Seinkönnens*]." *Sein und Zeit*, p. 144 (E.T., p. 184). Translation slightly altered.

[8]*Sein und Zeit*, p. 41 (E.T., p. 67).

[9]"That which is accessible [*das Gekannte*] in understanding as existential is no what, but instead being as existing. In the understanding lies existentially the manner of being of Dasein as being-able-to-be. Dasein is not something present-at-hand, which yet possesses whatever ability it has as something

in addition. On the contrary, it is primarily being-possible.
Dasein is in every case that which it can be, and it is how it
is its possibility." *Sein und Zeit*, p. 143 (E.T., p. 183).
Translation altered.

[10]"Higher than actuality stands possibility." *Sein und
Zeit*, p. 38 (E.T., p. 63). Also: "As a modal category of the
present-at-hand, possibility signifies what is *not yet* actual,
and what is *not ever* necessary. It characterizes the *merely*
possible. It is ontologically on a lower level than possibility
and necessity. On the contrary, however, possibility as existential is the most primordial and finally positive ontological
determinateness of Dasein." *Sein und Zeit*, pp. 143-144 (E.T.,
p. 183). Translation altered.

[11]"That wherein Dasein understands itself beforehand in the
mode of assigning itself is that upon which beings are already
allowed to be encountered. The 'wherein' of the understanding
that assigns itself as that upon which beings are allowed to be
encountered in the manner of being of involvement is the phenomenon of World. And the structure of that upon which Dasein
assigns itself is what constitutes the *worldhood* of the world."
Sein und Zeit, p. 86 (E.T., p. 119). Translation altered.

[12]"We name that *upon which* Dasein as such transcends 'the
world'." Martin Heidegger, *Vom Wesen des Grundes*, incorporated
in *The Essence of Reasons* (Evanston: Northwestern University
Press, 1969), p. 40.

[13]"Understanding of being is itself a determination of the
being of Dasein [*eine Seinsbestimmtheit des Daseins*]. The ontic
distinctiveness of Dasein lies in the fact the Dasein *is* ontological." *Sein und Zeit*, p. 12 (cf., E.T., p. 32). My translation.

[14]"Man is obviously a being [*etwas seiendes*]. As such he
belongs within the totality of being, just like the stone, the
tree, or the eagle....But what is distinctive of man is that he,
as the being [*Wesen*] who thinks, is open to being, is set before
being, remains related to being and thus is in accord with it.
Man *is* essentially this relation of being-in-accord [*dieser
Bezug der Entsprechung*], and he is only this." Martin Heidegger,
Identität und Differenz (Pfullingen: Gunther Neske, 1957),
p. 22 (cf. E.T.: *Identity and Difference*, trans. Joan Stambaugh
[New York: Harper & Row, 1969], p. 31). My translation. See
also Martin Heidegger, *Einführung in die Metaphysik* (Tübingen:
Niemeyer, 1953), p. 130 (E.T.: *An Introduction to Metaphysics*
[New York: Doubleday and Co., Anchor Books, 1961], p. 142).

[15]"We ask about the relation between human being and the
beings of beings. But--as soon as I thoughtfully say 'human
being,' I have already thereby said relatedness to being. Likewise, as soon as I thoughtfully say 'being of beings,' relatedness to human being has already thereby been named. In each of
the two parties of the relation between human being and being,
there already lies the relation itself." Martin Heidegger, *Was
Heisst Denken* (Tübingen: Niemeyer, 1954), p. 74 (cf., E.T.:
What is Called Thinking?, trans. Fred D. Wieck and J. Glenn Gray
[New York: Harper & Row, Harper Torchbook, 1972], p. 79). My
translation. See also: Martin Heidegger, *Zur Seinsfrage*

(Frankfurt am Main: Vittorio Klostermann, 1956), pp. 27-31
(E.T.: *The Question of Being*, trans. Jean Wilde and William
Kluback [New Haven: College and University Press, 1958], pp. 77-
85; and Martin Heidegger, "Brief Über den Humanismus," *Wegmarken*
(Frankfurt am Main: Vittorio Klostermann, 1967), p. 163 (E.T.:
"Letter on Humanism," trans. Frank Capuzzi and J. Glenn Gray, in
Martin Heidegger, *Basic Writings*, ed. David F. Krell [New York:
Harper & Row, 1977], p. 211).

[16]"The question concerning the relation of both [being and
man] has revealed itself to be inadequate, because it never
arrives in the domain of that which it seeks to question. In
truth, then, we can no longer even say that 'being' and 'man'
'are' [*seien*] the same in the sense that *they* belong together,
for to speak in *this* way is still to let each of these be for
itself." *Zur Seinsfrage*, p. 28 (cf., E.T., p. 77). My translation. Because of Heidegger's insistence that the relatedness of
being and man is primary with respect to both "parties" of the
relation, he also rejects all attempts to conceive the relation
in terms of a dialectic movement played between the two parties.
See, e.g., *Was Heisst Denken*, p. 74 (E.T., pp. 79-80).

[17]In Heidegger's later writings, he frequently hyphenates
the term "Da-sein" so that it says at once both human ek-sistence
and the "here" or locus of the emergence of being. Although we
leave the term "Da-sein" untranslated, we do occasionally translate the "*Da*" of this term as the "here" rather than the "there"
of being. We do this to show that the "place" of the emergence
of being is neither locationally specific nor at *any* distance
from human being, implications which are not clear if the "*Da*"
of Da-sein is translated with the usual "there." On the hyphen-
ation of "Da-sein" see, for example, "Brief über den Humanismus,"
pp. 156-158 (E.T., pp. 204-207). Note especially the following
statement: "Da-sein itself, however, prevails [*west*] as what is
'thrown.' It occurs in the throw of being which issues forth as
destiny [*des schickend Geschicklichen*]." (p. 158; cf., E.T.,
p. 207). My translation.

[18]Martin Heidegger, "Einleitung zu: 'Was ist Metaphysik?',"
in *Wegmarken*, p. 202 (cf., E.T.: "The Way Back into the Ground
of Metaphysics," in *Existentialism from Dostoevsky to Sartre*,
ed. and trans. Walter Kaufmann [New York: Meridian Books, 1956],
p. 213). My translation.

[19]*Zur Seinsfrage*, p. 17 (E.T., p. 55). Also: "Dasein says:
care of the being of beings as such, being as ecstatically manifest in Dasein. Dasein is thus not merely care of human being.
Dasein is 'in every case mine,' but this means neither posited
by me nor relegated to an individual self. Dasein is *itself* by
virtue of its essential relation to being in general. This is
the meaning of the sentence that occurs frequently in *Sein und
Zeit*: 'There belongs to Dasein an understanding of being.'"
Einführung in die Metaphysik, p. 22 (cf., E.T., p. 24). My
translation.

[20]See *Sein und Zeit*, pp. 212-230 (E.T., pp. 256-273). Note
especially the following passage: "Disclosedness is the fundamental character of Dasein, in accord with which Dasein *is* its
'here' [*Da*]....Insofar as Dasein *is* essentially its disclosedness

and as something disclosed discloses and uncovers, it is essentially 'true.' *Dasein is 'in the truth.'"* Ibid., pp. 220-221 (cf., E.T., p. 263). Italics original, my translation.

[21]*Zur Seinsfrage*, p. 21 (cf., E.T., p. 63). My translation.

[22]*Was Heisst Denken?*, p. 77 (cf., E.T., p. 98). My translation.

[23]"[The definitive interpretation of being which was secured in the word *ousia*] means being in the sense of permanent presence, being already present [*Vorhandenheit*]. What is really in being is thus the being that always is, *aei on*. What is permanently present is what we must go back to in all comprehending and producing, the standard, the *idea*....Seen in relation to *physis*, to emergence, what always lies before is the *proteron*, the earlier, the *a-priori*." *Einführung in die Metaphysik*, p. 147 (cf., E.T., p. 161). My translation.

[24]Martin Heidegger, *Zur Sache des Denkens* (Tübingen: Max Niemeyer, 1969), p. 62 (E.T.: *On Time and Being*, trans. Joan Stambaugh [New York: Harper & Row, 1972], p. 56).

[25]*Was Heisst Denken?*, p. 174 (E.T., p. 227).

[26]"Thought with respect to what is present [*das Anwesende*], coming-to-presence [*Anwesen*] shows itself as letting-come-to-presence [*Anwesenlassen*]. *Zur Sache des Denkens*, p. 5 (cf., E.T., p. 5). My translation.

[27]Ibid., p. 40 (E.T., p. 37). Translation altered.

[28]"What is present has emerged out of unconcealment....Its coming-to-presence is an emerging entry into what is concealed within unconcealment...." *Was Heisst Denken?*, p. 144 (cf., E.T., p. 236). My translation.

[29]"But if letting-come-to-presence is thought on its own terms then what is involved in this letting is no longer *what* is present but coming-to-presence itself....*Only because there prevails [es gibt] an allowance of coming to presence is the letting-come-to-presence of what is present possible.*" (Italics original.) *Zur Sache des Denkens*, p. 40 (cf., E.T., p. 37). My translation.

[30]*Zur Sache des Denkens*, p. 75 (cf., E.T., p. 68). My translation.

[31]*Zur Sache des Denkens*, p. 12 (cf., E.T., p. 12). My translation. See also *Zur Seinsfrage*, p. 28 (E.T., p. 77).

[32]*Sein und Zeit*, p. 42 (E.T., p. 67).

[33]"Brief über den 'humanismus'," pp. 156-157 (cf., E.T., pp. 206-207). My translation.

[34]"Bauen Wohnen Denken," in *Vorträge und Aufsätze*, Teil II, pp. 28-33 (E.T.: "Building Dwelling Thinking" in *Poetry, Language, Thought*, pp. 154-159).

[35] Ibid., p. 31 (E.T., p. 156). Translation altered slightly.

[36] "Bauen Wohnen Denken," p. 31 (E.T., pp. 156-157). Translation altered.

[37] Ibid., pp. 31-32 (E.T., p. 157). Translation altered.

[38] "Brief über den 'Humanismus'," pp. 155-162 (E.T., pp. 202-208).

[39] *Zur Seinsfrage*, p. 38 (cf., E.T., p. 97). My translation.

[40] *Einführung in die Metaphysik*, pp. 124-125 (cf., E.T., p. 137). My translation. See also the following passage: "Dasein is the unremitting yet perilous necessity of defeat and of renewed acts of violence against being. At the abode of its appearing, the supreme power of being literally violates, rapes Dasein. As this abode, being encompasses and permeates Dasein and thereby holds it in being." Ibid., p. 136 (cf., E.T., p. 149). My translation.

[41] The entire passage reads: "Thought in terms of ek-sistence, world is in a certain fashion precisely the 'beyond' [*das Jenseitige*] within and for ek-sistence. Man is never at first a subject on this side of the world, whether this subject be taken as 'I' or as 'we.' He is also never at first only a subject that is always at the same time related to objects, so that his essence resides in the subject-object relation. Much rather is man before all this in his essence ek-sistent in the openness of being, which openness first illumines the 'between' within which a 'relation' of subject to object can 'be.'" "Brief über den 'Humanismus'," pp. 180-181 (cf., E.T., p. 229). My translation.

[42] "Die Zeit des Weltbildes," in *Holzwege*, p. 83 (cf., E.T.: "The Age of the World Picture," in *The Question Concerning Technology*, trans. W. Lovitt [New York: Harper & Row, Harper Colophon Books, 1977], p. 131). My translation.

[43] "Letting oneself enter in upon the unconcealedness of beings is not to lose oneself in them but is rather what transpires in a stepping back in the face of beings, so that they may reveal themselves as what and how they are, in order that representative assimilation may take its standard from them. As this letting-be, it sets itself out before beings as such and so transposes all its determinate relations into the open. Letting-be, i.e., freedom, is intrinsically a setting-itself-out-beyond, ek-sistent...freedom reveals itself to be the setting-itself-out into the unconcealedness of beings." "Vom Wesen der Wahrheit," in *Wegmarken*, p. 84 (cf., E.T.: "On the Essence of Truth," in Heidegger, *Basic Writings*, p. 128). My translation.

[44] The original discussion of *Entschlossenheit* is to be found in section 60 of *Sein und Zeit*, pp. 295-301 (E.T., pp. 341-348).

[45] See *Einführung in die Metaphysik*, p. 16 (E.T., p. 17).

[46]See the discussion of *Verfallensein* in *Sein und Zeit*,
pp. 175-180 (E.T., pp. 219-224). See also "Vom Wesen der
Wahrheit," pp. 89-91 (E.T., pp. 130-132).

[47]"Der Ursprung des Kunstwerkes," p. 55 (cf., E.T., p. 67).
My translation.

[48]"As the letting-be of beings, freedom is intrinsically
the open relation [*das entschlossene Verhältnis*] that does not
close itself off." "Vom Wesen der Wahrheit," p. 90 (cf., E.T.,
p. 133). My translation.

[49]See "Nachwort zu: 'Was ist Metaphysik?'," in *Wegmarken*,
p. 106 (E.T.: "Postscript" to "What is Metaphysics?," in Martin
Heidegger, *Existence and Being*, ed. Werner Brock, trans. R. Hull
and A. Crick [Chicago: Henry Regnery Co., Gateway ed., 1970],
pp. 359-360). See also: "Der Urspring des Kunstwerkes," p. 55
(E.T., pp. 67-68).

[50]"Einleitung zu: Was ist Metaphysik?," p. 203 (cf., E.T.,
p. 214). My translation.

[51]Found in *Identität und Differenz*, pp. 11-34 (E.T., pp. 21-
41).

[52]*Identität und Differenz*, pp. 18-19 (E.T., pp. 27-28). See
also: *Einführung in die Metaphysik*, pp. 104-112 (E.T., pp. 115-
123); and *Was Heisst Denken?*, pp. 147-148 (E.T., pp. 240-242).

[53]*Identität und Differenz*, pp. 19-21 (E.T., pp. 28-29).

[54]*Einführung in die Metaphysik*, pp. 124, 125, 134 (cf.,
E.T., pp. 136-137, 138, 147). Translations mine.

[55]"Nachwort zu: 'Was ist Metaphysik?'," p. 105 (cf., E.T.,
pp. 357-358). Translation mine.

[56]*Einführung in die Metaphysik*, p. 11 (E.T., pp. 11-12).

[57]It should be kept in mind that such "sacrifice" is not a
volitional accomplishment on the part of any human individual.
"The origin of sacrifice is in the essence of the enowning
transpiration [*Ereignis*] as which being claims man for the truth
of being." "Nachwort zu: 'Was ist Metaphysik?'," p. 106 (cf.,
E.T., p. 359). Translation mine.

[58]The most extensive discussion of "gathering" is to be
found in two of the essays in *Vorträge und Aufsätze*, Teil II.
They are "Bauen Wohnen Denken" (pp. 19-36; E.T., pp. 141-161),
and "Das Ding" (pp. 37-55; E.T., pp. 163-186). In these essays
it is the thing which gathers the fourfold region of all coming-
to-presence, the region in which human dwelling essentially
occurs. But it should be noted here that the term "thing" does
not name for Heidegger the *particularity* of a thing, i.e., its
determinate presentment in terms of specific properties and
features, but rather the world-extensive tissue of meaning-
allowances as which the being of the thing transpires. Gathering is thus focused in the thing in *this* sense, and as such,

gathering is the underlying relatedness that already joins ek-sistence to the coming-to-presence of what is present. See especially *Vorträge und Aufsätze*, Teil II, pp. 26-32 and 45-50 (E.T., pp. 151-158 and 177-182).

[59]"Brief über den Humanismus," p. 163 (cf., E.T., p. 211). My translation.

[60]*Was Heisst Denken?*, p. 157 (cf., E.T., p. 144). My translation.

[61]For Heidegger's discussion of these overtones, see *Zur Sache des Denkens*, pp. 71-72 (E.T., p. 65).

[62]"[The clearing is what] gives free reign, where all that is cleared and freed, and all that conceals itself, together attain the open freedom." *Unterwegs zur Sprache*. Pfullingen: Neske, 1959, p. 197 (E.T., *On the Way to Language*, trans. Peter Hertz. [New York: Harper & Row, 1971], p. 91).

[63]*Zur Sache des Denkens*, p. 72 (cf., E.T., p. 65). My translation.

[64]"Whether or not what is present is experienced, grasped or presented, presence as an abiding in openness always remains dependent upon the *Lichtung*." Ibid., pp. 73-74 (E.T., p. 67). Translation altered.

[65]"Der Ursprung des Kunstwerkes," p. 41 (cf., E.T., p. 53). My translation.

[66]"Der Ursprung des Kunstwerkes," p. 42 (cf., E.T., p. 53). My translation.

[67]*Zur Sache des Denkens*, p. 75 (cf., E.T., p. 68). My translation.

[68]There are several passages in which Heidegger attempts to push through to this "grant" itself by musing over the peculiarly German expression "*Es gibt Sein*." The usual translation of this statement would be: "There is being." Heidegger, however, takes the statement with unidiomatic literalness to say: "It gives being." He then asks concerning the "It" which "gives" being, and in this manner seeks to give thought to *Lichtung* as such. See, e.g., *Zur Sache des Denkens*, pp. 4-6 (E.T., pp. 5-6); and "Brief über den Humanismus," pp. 165-169 (E.T., pp. 213-217).

[69]*Identität und Differenz*, pp. 22-23 (E.T., p. 31). Translation altered.

[70]*Identität und Differenz*, p. 24 (E.T., p. 32).

[71]"Vom Wesen der Wahrheit," p. 87f (E.T., pp. 130-132).

[72]"Was ist Metaphysik?," in *Wegmarken*, pp. 1-7 (E.T.: "What is Metaphysics?," in *Basic Writings*, pp. 95-104). It should be kept in mind that the term "*das Nichts*" is not intended as a final characterization of this primordial realm, but is instead a preliminary designation of the "path" that a

thoughtful pursuit must take which seeks to enter this realm.
The term "Nothing," "*das Nichts*," is preliminary because it
designates this realm *not* in terms of this realm itself but
instead in terms of its *difference* from beings, from what is.
Thus it names the primordial realm only in a relative, preliminary way.

[73]"Was ist Metaphysik?," p. 9 (cf., E.T., p. 103). My
translation.

[74]Ibid., p. 8f (E.T., p. 102f).

[75]Ibid., p. 9 (cf., E.T., p. 103). My translation.

[76]Was ist Metaphysik?," p. 10f (cf., E.T., p. 104). My
translation.

[77]Ibid., p. 11 (cf., E.T., p. 105). My translation.

[78]"Vom Wesen der Wahrheit," pp. 89, 91 (cf., E.T., pp. 133,
135). My translation.

CHAPTER IV

NOTES

[1] "Das Ding," p. 41 (E.T., p. 169). Translation altered.

[2] "Das Ding," pp. 41-43 (E.T., pp. 169-171).

[3] "Das Ding," p. 44 (E.T., pp. 171-172). Translation slightly altered.

[4] "Das Ding," pp. 45-46 (E.T., p. 173). Translation slightly altered.

[5] See "Die Ursprung des Kunstwerkes," pp. 34-36 (E.T., pp. 45-47).

[6] "Das Ding," p. 51 (E.T., pp. 178-179). Translation altered.

[7] "Das Ding," p. 52 (E.T., p. 179). Translation altered.

[8] The phrase "to pay attention" implicitly recognizes that one is *claimed* by that which is to be attended to, and thus that one *owes* to it one's attention.

[9] The only mode of awareness in which beings fail to lay claim is *Angst*, as we have seen at the end of Chapter III.

[10] See "...dichterisch wohnet der Mensch...." in *Vorträge und Aufsätze*, Teil II, pp. 71-72 (E.T., "...Poetically man Dwells...." in *Poetry, Language, Thought*, p. 123).

[11] See our earlier discussion of overwhelmingness and the "nothingness" of human ek-sistence which this entails, on pp. 82-83.

[12] In this discussion we see reflected the etymology of the word "transcendence" itself, which as we saw much earlier indicates that the movement of surpassing fixed limit or boundary metes out a measure for the one (man) who follows along the path of the movement. See above, pp. 4-5.

[13] Two essays in which the danger threatening Da-sein is discussed are "Die Frage nach der Technik," in *Vorträge und Aufsätze*, Teil I, pp. 5-36, and also in *Die Technik und die Kehre* (Pfullingen: Gunther Neske, 1962), pp. 5-36 (E.T., "The Question Concerning Technology," in *The Question Concerning Technology and Other Essays*, trans. William Lovitt [New York: Harper & Row, 1977], pp. 3-35); and "Der Satz der Identität," in *Identität and Differenz*, pp. 11-34 (E.T., *Identity and Differ- ence*, pp. 23-41). A third essay, "Die Gefahr" ("The Danger"), written in 1949, has unfortunately remained unpublished as far as this writer knows.

[14]We must "bracket" for the present the question of the relation of the previous fourfold account of world-openness to the account that now ensues. See below, pp. 124-126.

[15]See above, p. 93.

[16]*Identität und Differenz*, p. 25 (E.T., p. 33).

[17]*Identität und Differenz*, pp. 25f (E.T., pp. 30f).

[18]For a discussion of the meaning of "*Wesen*," see "Die Frage nach der Technik," pp. 30f (E.T., pp. 30f).

[19]Ibid., p. 5 (E.T., p. 4).

[20]"Die Frage nach der Technik," p. 16. (E.T., p. 16.) Concerning the translation of *stellen* and its cognates, see note 14, Ibid., p. 15.

[21]Ibid., p. 16 (cf., E.T., p. 17). Translation altered. For a discussion of the term "*Bestand*," particularly in connection with the usurpation of ek-sistence by the will to power, see "Nietzsches Wort 'Gott ist tot'," in *Holzwege*, p. 221 (E.T., "The Word of Nietzsche: 'God is Dead'," *The Question Concerning Technology*, p. 84).

[22]*Identität und Differenz*, pp. 25-27 (E.T., pp. 33-35).

[23]"Die Frage nach der Technik," p. 24 (E.T., p. 24). Translation altered slightly. See also Ibid., pp. 31-32 (E.T., pp. 31-32).

[24]*Identität und Differenz*, p. 27 (E.T., p. 35). Translation altered.

[25]Ibid., p. 27 (E.T., p. 35); *Vorträge und Aufsätze*, Teil I, p. 19 (E.T., p. 19).

[26]"Die Frage nach der Technik," p. 27 (E.T., p. 27). Emphasis added, my translation.

[27]"Die Kehre," in *Die Technik und die Kehre*, p. 37 (E.T., "The Turning," in *The Question Concerning Technology*, pp. 36-37). Translation altered slightly.

[28]By speaking both of gathering-into-orderability and of the fourfold of meaning each as essential characterizations of Da-sein, two things are indicated. First, the thoroughgoing historicity of Da-sein is indicated, i.e., that Da-sein *is* solely *how* it emerges. And secondly, gathering-into-orderability is shown to characterize Da-sein not simply in "the technological age," but rather throughout the history of the West. However, this destiny is *peculiarly* associated with the technological age in that its essential trait, the orderability of everything, comes to an overbearing hegemony in the modern technological world. Nonetheless, whenever there occurred the tendency to reduce the coming-to-presence of anything to its *determinate* and hence fully available presentment, even in pre-technological eras, there gathering-into-orderability is manifest.

[29] We have enclosed the word "transcendent" in inverted commas in order to indicate once again that this term does not here mean non-emergent reality separated from human ek-sistence, but rather means the non-surpassable emergence of articulated world which is given as the foundational preserve of human dwelling.

[30] "Die Kehre," p. 40 (E.T., p. 41). See also *Identität und Differenz*, pp. 32-33 (E.T., p. 40).

[31] "Die Kehre," p. 42 (E.T., p. 43). Translation altered.

[32] "Die Kehre," p. 43 (E.T., p. 44). Translation altered.

[33] *Identität und Differenz*, pp. 28-34 (E.T., pp. 36-41).

[34] *Unterwegs zur Sprache*, p. 258 (E.T., p. 127). See the entire discussion, pp. 256-268 (E.T., pp. 125-136).

[35] *Zur Sache des Denkens*, p. 24 (E.T., p. 24). See pp. 19-25 (E.T., pp. 19-24) for another discussion of *Er-Eignis*.

[36] This term is coined by Albert Hofstadter in his excellent article on *Er-Eignis* entitled "Enownment," *Boundary II* IV, 2 (Winter, 1976), pp. 357-377.

[37] "Die Kehre," p. 44 (E.T., p. 45). See also *Identität und Differenz*, pp. 28-29.

[38] See "Die Kehre," pp. 44-45 (E.T., pp. 46-47); *Unterwegs zur Sprache*, p. 264 (E.T., p. 133); *Identität und Differenz*, pp. 28-29.

[39] "Die Kehre," pp. 46-47 (E.T., p. 49). Translation slightly altered.

SELECTED BIBLIOGRAPHY

German Works of Heidegger

Einführung in die Metaphysik. Tübingen: Niemeyer, 1953.

Gelassenheit. Pfullingen: Neske, 1959.

Holzwege. Frankfurt am Main: Klostermann, 1950.

Identität und Differenz. Pfullingen: Neske, 1957.

Zur Sache des Denkens. Tübingen: Niemeyer, 1969.

Zur Seinsfrage. Frankfurt am Main: Klostermann, 1956.

Sein und Zeit. 12th ed. Tübingen: Niemeyer, 1972.

Die Technik und die Kehre. Pfullingen: Neske, 1962.

Unterwegs zur Sprache. Tübingen: Neske, 1959.

Vorträge und Aufsätze. 3 Vols. Tübingen: Neske, 1967.

Was Heisst Denken? Tübingen: Niemeyer, 1954.

Wegmarken. Frankfurt am Main: Klostermann, 1967.

Vom Wesen des Grundes. Frankfurt am Main: Klostermann, 1929.

English Translations of Heidegger's Works

Basic Writings, ed. David Krell. New York: Harper & Row, 1977.

Being and Time, trans. John Macquarrie and Edward Robinson. New York: Harper & Row, 1962 (translation of *Sein und Zeit*).

Discourse on Thinking, trans. John Anderson and E. Hans Freund. New York: Harper & Row, 1966; Harper Torchbooks, 1969 (translation of *Gelassenheit*).

The Essence of Reasons, trans. Terrence Malick. Evanston: Northwestern University Press, 1969 (translation of *Vom Wesen des Grundes*).

Existence and Being, trans. R. Hull and Alan Crick. Chicago: Henry Regnery, Gateway Edition, 1949.

Identity and Difference, trans. Joan Stambaugh. New York: Harper & Row, 1969 (translation of *Identität und Differenz*).

An Introduction to Metaphysics, trans. Ralph Manheim. New York:
    Doubleday and Co., Anchor Books, 1961 (translation of
    Einführung in die Metaphysik).

On Time and Being, trans. Joan Stambaugh. New York: Harper &
    Row, 1972 (translation of *Zur Sache des Denkens*).

On the Way to Language, trans. Peter Hertz. New York: Harper
    & Row, 1971 (translation of *Unterwegs zur Sprache*).

Poetry, Language, Thought, trans. Albert Hofstadter. New York:
    Harper & Row, 1971.

The Question Concerning Technology, trans. William Lovitt. New
    York: Harper & Row, 1977.

The Question of Being, trans. Jean Wilde and William Kluback.
    New Haven: College and University Press, 1958 (translation
    of *Zur Seinsfrage*).

"The Way Back into the Ground of Metaphysics," in *Existentialism
    from Dostoevsky to Sartre*, ed. and trans. Walter Kaufmann.
    New York: The World Publishing Co., Meridian Books, 1956.

What is Called Thinking?, trans. Fred Wieck and J. Glenn Gray.
    New York: Harper & Row, 1968; Harper Torchbooks, 1972.

                              Other Works

Bonhoeffer, Dietrich. *Letters and Papers from Prison.* New
    York: Macmillan Co., 1971.

The Collected Dialogues of Plato. Edited by Edith Hamilton and
    Huntington Cairns. Bollingen Series LXXI. New York:
    Pantheon Books, 1961.

Gadamer, Hans Georg. *Philosophical Hermeneutics*, trans. and
    Introduction by David E. Linge. Berkeley: University of
    California Press, 1976.

_____. *Truth and Method.* New York: The Seabury Press,
    1975 (translation of *Wahrheit und Methode*).

_____. *Wahrheit und Methode*, 3rd ed. Tübingen: J.C.B.
    Mohr, 1972.

Hofstadter, Albert. "Enownment." *Boundary II* 4 (Winter
    1976): 357-377.

Marx, Werner. *Heidegger and the Tradition*, trans. Theodore
    Kisiel and Murray Greene. Evanston: Northwestern
    University Press, 1971.

Palmer, Richard E. *Hermeneutics.* Evanston: Northwestern
    University Press, 1969.

Die Religion in Geschichte und Gegenwart, 3rd ed., s.v.
  "Transcendenz und Immanenz," by H. Blumenberg.

Richardson, William J. *Heidegger: Through Phenomenology to
  Thought*, 2nd ed. The Hague: Nijhoff, 1967.

Tillich, Paul. *The Protestant Era*. Chicago: University of
  Chicago Press, 1948; Phoenix Books, abridged ed., 1957.

Whitehead, Alfred North. *Process and Reality*. New York:
  The Macmillan Co., 1929, 1957.

Wittgenstein, Ludwig. *Philosophical Investigations*. New York:
  The Macmillan Co., 1953.

_____. *Tractatus Logico-Philosophicus*. London: Routledge
  and Kegan Paul, 1922.